OFF TO A GOOD START

A Manual for
Raising Your New Puppy

Mary Thompson

ADAMS MEDIA

Avon, Massachusetts

Published by
Adams Media, an F+W Publications Company
57 Littlefield Street, Avon, MA 02322. U.S.A.
www.adamsmedia.com

ISBN: 1-58062-217-8

Printed in Canada.

J I H G F E D

Library of Congress Cataloging-in-Publication Data

Thompson, Mary (Mary E.)
Off to a good start : a manual for raising your new puppy / Mary Thompson
p.   cm.
ISBN 1-58062-217-8
1. Puppies Handbooks, manuals, etc. 2. Dogs Handbooks, manuals, etc.
I. Title. II. Title: Manual for raising your new puppy.
SF427.T48   1999
636.7'0887—dc21   99-26460
CIP

This publication is designed to provide accurate and authoritative information
with regard to the subject matter covered. It is sold with the understanding that
the publisher is not engaged in rendering legal, accounting, or other professional advice. If legal advice or other expert assistance is required, the services
of a competent professional person should be sought.
  — From a *Declaration of Principles* jointly adopted by a Committee of the
American Bar Association and a Committee of Publishers and Associations

Cover photo by Gary J. Lamarre
Inside illustrations by Betty Mueller and Barry Littmann

*This book is available at quantity discounts for bulk purchases.
For information, call 1-800-872-5627.*

Contents

Foreword

A puppy—an adorable creature designed to wiggle into your heart. A puppy—hopes and dreams in an irresistible package.

What are your dreams for your pup? World-class companion welcomed by all your friends and family? Show dog? Therapy dog? Top performance dog wow-ing everyone with their abilities in dog sports? All of the above?

Hopefully, you've done your homework and have found a pup bred for health and temperament who was raised with maximum socialization. Or maybe you've given a home to a stray or pound puppy or have fallen in love with a pet shop puppy, or, as I did once, bought a pup from a breeder more interested in bucks than the lives of the pups (these people range from top show breeders to back-yard breeders and puppy mills).

No matter where your pup has come from, Mary Thompson's *Off to a Good Start* will tell you how to realize your dreams—to have a dog who makes you proud, a dog whose manners and training enable him to have a life with freedom, fun, and the full companionship of you and your family. The information in this book is based on extensive research, continual reading of dog-related literature and YEARS of raising and training dogs. Nothing you will find here is based on far-fetched ideas or unproved theories. Mary's knowledge comes from time-tested experience.

Since 1990, I have been running Camp Gone to the Dogs— Vermont Vacations for Dog Lovers and Their Dogs. Mary has been with me every step of the way, giving hundreds of campers the benefit of her knowledge. I receive letters from grateful campers all year long telling me that what they've learned from Mary has often dramatically changed their dog's health and behavior. She is incredibly generous with her time and knowledge and often touches on many subjects typically not covered by other trainers or books.

Socializing your dog to other dogs is one such topic. At every camp we've had unhappy campers who learned in that setting that their dog could not tolerate the company of other dogs. Had these people had access to Mary's instruction when they brought their pup home, they would have had an entirely different experience. It's a real shame when a dog does not get along with other dogs.

This comprehensive book is based on common sense and practical suggestions. If you follow Mary's advice, you'll be the envy of other dog owners, having a canine companion you can enjoy to the max. A good dog is one of life's great pleasures.

I know my campers will be thrilled to have Mary "in writing" and I plan on giving a copy of *Off to a Good Start* to anyone who buys a pup from me.

—Honey Loring, M.A.Ed.
Founder and Director, Camp Gone to the Dogs

Acknowledgments

The author would like to take this time to thank those people and dogs who contributed so much to the making of this book.

Ronald and Cora Goodwin, my parents, for never saying, "Enough animals!" Ross W. Thompson, DVM, my husband, for help with the medical advice and, like my parents, for never saying "NO" to one more animal coming into the house. Andrew and Adam Thompson, our sons, for giving me another viewpoint on how to raise and train our pups.

Laurie Downs, who is always there when I need her—for help with my animals, my children, my sanity, and for reading, rereading, and rereading again the manuscript and making those subtle but necessary changes—thank you for knowing what I wanted to say but hadn't! To her husband, Steven Downs, for building my scent hurdle equipment, flyball box, and agility equipment so that I can have fun with my dogs. Barbara

Hooper, Lorraine Tighe, Sandy Robinson, Renae Peterson, friends who took the time to critique the manuscript, help with grammatical errors, and suggest some thoughts I had not considered before. Beth True, a vet in the making, for reading the first rough draft and lending credence to the endeavor.

Betty Mueller for publishing the original spiral-bound version of this book and designing its cover, thank you for all of your help through the years. Adam Thompson for the drawings for the original book, at 14 he is as good a cartoonist as he is a dog trainer. Would that I had had his knowledge at that age!

More friends who have been a big influence on what I do and how I do it:

Honey Loring, founder of Camp Gone to the Dogs—you, the other instructors, and the campers have all contributed to help me see differently, thank you!

Colleen and Jack McDaniel and their staff at the Academy of Canine Behavior, who have all listened to me, let me try to teach them new ideas, and turned around and taught me, thank you.

To Susan Rickwood and Margaret Schneider, thank you for the last revisions, for working so close to the deadline—with lives of your own!

Leslie McGuirk, a friend indeed who gave a copy of the original puppy book to a friend—Cheryl Kimball of Adams Media Corporation. Thank you both for seeing validity in the first manuscript!

Lastly and mostly, to the dogs I have lived with, laughed, loved and cried for, who taught me so very much—Mitzi, J.J., Matty, Seymour, Jamie, Jessie, Storm, Cory, Suni, Flint, Kaitlin, Kate, Hank, Aaron, Chip, Rain, Morgan, Erin, Ten, Lacy, Joy, Tango, and Danny.

Introduction

This book was put together as an aid to raise your puppy and to help you make decisions concerning the dog and your family. This is not a training book; rather it is a book that gives you choices on how to raise your puppy. After more than thirty-two years of experience raising and training dogs, I still believe that the way I trained my dog when I was fourteen is the best—with love, treats, and lots of praise.

Any medical/health information should not take the place of your veterinarian's advice. There are a number of good books that cover most of these topics in greater detail. Check the suggested reading list at the back.

There will always be days when you doubt your sanity for getting a puppy. Relax. It happens to all of us. Just remember why you got a dog in the first place—as a friend and companion, as a hunter, as an obedience dog, as an agility dog, to breed, show, or work.

Every pup has the potential to be everything you want it to be. It is up to you to harness this potential and make your puppy into the kind of dog you are proud of. It takes work, time, and patience to raise a dog right. Then, again, nothing worth having in life is free and easy. The amount of effort you expend to raise your puppy properly will reflect in how he or she behaves. The more time you invest, the better the dog!

Temperament has to do with the cards you are dealt; training and socialization are how you play them. Behavior is the effect of training and socialization on temperament. Most puppies are not born mean or vicious; it is what they become without proper management, training, and socialization from their owners! However, puppies **ARE** heavily influenced by their mothers, so if you are thinking of getting a puppy whose mother is shy or fearful or even aggressive toward people, be forewarned that some of that attitude has already rubbed off onto her puppies. You either should avoid getting a puppy from that litter or be prepared to spend a lot of time, effort, and patience to turn the puppy into a better adult than his mother.

A dog's love and friendship is a special gift. Enjoy it, nurture it, and return it. You can be your dog's best friend, just as he can be yours!

Chapter 1

Bringing Spike Home

The First Day

Congratulations on your new puppy! Just what does having a puppy mean and involve? Well, you are about to find out.

Your dog is a living, breathing creature. He is not meant to be tied up, to be left alone all day, or to sleep in the garage at night. By bringing this pup into your home, you accepted responsibility to raise him to be your companion. By reading this book, taking puppy classes taught by a good instructor, and getting extra help when needed, you can raise a great dog that everyone admires and wishes they had.

Spike's body and mind need exercise and stimulation just as ours do, so *you* may be getting more exercise (both mentally and physically) than you first planned on. If you are bringing home a puppy between the ages of seven and sixteen weeks, remember that he is still an infant. A pup is like a baby who has just started to crawl; the whole world is out there to explore. Just like a baby, Spike needs a safe, secure home with caring people to watch over him. The way you handle the pup, and any problems or situations that arise, will set the tone for your entire relationship.

Before going to get Spike from the breeder/previous owner, take a few moments to plan how the first few days will be for the pup and his new family. Ask the person you are getting Spike from if he/she will put a small towel, fleece toy, or rope in with the pup so that the item will have time to get scented by his current surroundings. The object will hold familiar smells for Spike when he goes to his new home and might help him be less stressed. If possible, send ahead one of your towels or offer to pay the current owner to purchase something for the pup ahead of time. Also find out what the pup is eating so that you can have the same brand on hand. Changing the pup's diet as soon as he gets to his new home can give him diarrhea, making house-training that much more difficult. Ask if the pup has been given milk before. If not, avoid milk when you get home; it too can cause diarrhea.

When you are ready to get Spike, try to do so as early in the day as possible. This way, he'll have some time to get used to his new home before nighttime. If Spike has the chance to have a meal or two in his new home before bedtime, he might not mind the absence of his littermates and old familiar sounds and smells as much. Plus he will be tired, full, and ready for sleep. After having a few naps in his new home, he'll be more used to it and less upset over leaving his previous place. He may cry less during the first night if he has had a full day to become accustomed to his new home.

If you have other animals at home, see if you can bathe Spike before bringing him home, using one of the shampoos you normally use on the other animals. Dry him off using your own towels. This way he'll smell more like your home, and the other animals may accept him faster, as he won't smell strange to them. If you don't have time or the option to bathe Spike before bringing him home, let him get used to his new home for a few hours without the other animals around. Than give him a bath and dry him off with one of the towels you regularly use on the other animals. This will help him blend in better with the household smells, and the other animals may not be as upset over having another new animal in the house.

Is someone going to hold him for the ride home? Or is he going to be put into a crate? Do not plan to go by yourself if you can help it. Trying to drive and hold Spike at the same time is just not safe. Ask a friend to come along, but pick someone who will not be too upset if the puppy either becomes carsick or urinates on him/her (this may be a test of true friendship). Obviously you will want to take along clean-up material in case of any accidents. While a crate would be safer, if he has not already been left in a crate for a short period of time, this could make him very frightened and stressed out—not the perfect ride to his new home, in his eyes at least. Once he is used to being in a crate, he'll feel comfortable being crated in the car.

In case the person you get the pup from does not provide him with a collar and leash, you need to take one with you. This way, if you should stop along the road to let him out, he'll be safe, rather than running around the car and into traffic. Even a collar that is a little snug (for the ride home) is better than one that is too loose and may slip off over his head. And it should be a buckle collar, not a choke collar, for a young pup.

Take some cloth towels, paper towels, and plastic bags to clean up and contain any messes. Try to pick up the pup in between feedings, and don't give him any water during the ride unless necessary. Adding carsickness on top of leaving his brothers, sisters, mom, and familiar place will have Spike wondering if he'll live to see the end of the ride.

When you bring the pup home (and he is the only animal), take him out to the yard to the area you want him to use as his toilet area. When he has gone to the bathroom, allow him to do some exploring of the yard. After a few minutes, take him into the house and let him explore on his own the areas that you will allow him into. Keep the children and other animals away from him for a while so that he can explore without being fearful. He'll need to go to the bathroom during this exploration, so you'll want to take him back to the toilet area at some point.

When he is brought back into the house, show him the water dish and give him a little bit of food to help him feel at home. If Spike acts afraid of being in his new home, lie down on the floor and encourage him to walk over you or cuddle with you. You are less threatening to him if you make yourself smaller. (The average-size eight-week-old Labrador retriever sees people in their true size from the person's feet up to their knees. From there on up, the person appears more than eight feet tall with a very small head, much like in the funny mirrors at a carnival or circus.)

Have the rest of the family sit on the floor and let Spike come to them. He may come bounding up to everyone, in which case he can be picked up and held. If he approaches slowly, just remind everyone to sit still and let Spike make the moves toward them. They should not reach toward him, as he will only back up out of reach. Reaching out suddenly to pick him up will scare him. In a few hours, he should be fine with the family; it just takes some puppies longer than others to feel comfortable with a new home, new smells, new people, new everything!

When you reach out to pat Spike, don't go for the top of his head. A pup reacts to anything going over the top of his head by ducking down his head or entire body. This is part of his survival instinct.

If Spike does duck his head when you reach out to pat him, talk to him and touch him on the front of his chest first. As he accepts this contact, still maintain your hand on his body and *GRADUALLY* massage your way up to his head, the side of his face, and neck area. This procedure will keep him from becoming hand shy. Have everyone touch Spike on his chest area first before touching other areas. He will gradually accept hands reaching out to him.

Pups need to nap frequently. If they are kept busy, they may become hyperactive. Once Spike has explored his new home, have everyone settle down and ignore him. If you block off the area that you are in with the pup, he'll eventually lie down and take a nap. As soon as he wakes up, he'll need to urinate! *Hurry* him outside and praise him when he goes. Pups play for fifteen to twenty minutes and then need a nap. Some pups will exhibit being overtired by whining or becoming more mouthy (nipping, biting, or grabbing).

The day you bring Spike home is not the day to have company. If you have children and they want their friends over to see the new puppy, ask them to wait a few days. Spike needs to learn who the family members are, his house, its smells, the boundaries, and so on. Having extra people over will only cause more confusion in his mind and stress him out more. And there is nothing more upsetting to a child than to have his or her new puppy act like it would rather be with one of the friends.

Where is he going to be kept when no one is around to watch over him? He may not do a lot of damage chewing on furniture in the beginning, but he will once his adult teeth come in! If you're going to keep him in a crate, what room will it be in? Being put in the family room might be okay if the children in the family will let him be and allow him to have some peace and quiet to sleep. Being put in the kitchen is okay also, as long as the crate is NOT right near the pathway of everyone walking by. This will keep him awake and deprive him of his rightful and necessary allotment of sleep. The basement may give him some time away from the family, but it will also show him that you want that distance maintained, and he might never bond strongly with you. Keeping the crate in the bedroom is much like keeping a crib in the bedroom. It works great for some people; for others it means sleepless nights.

You need to do what is right for you, your family, and your home. Planning ahead and deciding where the crate will go, which door the pup should use to go out to the toilet area, and so on, will help the pup feel more at home and settle in faster than moving his crate around every day until you figure out where you really want it to be. Similarly, choose one door as his "out" door. Taking him outside from one door and then another one the next time he needs to go out will confuse him and make house-training a longer process; he won't know which door he should start walking toward to let you know he needs to go out.

Introducing Spike to Your Other Dog

If you already have a dog (let's call him Rover) at home, have a friend or family member take the dog on a leash to a neutral spot away from his home and yard. Take the puppy out of the car on a leash also. Have the person holding Rover start walking toward you as you walk toward them, but the two of you should pass each other with over thirty feet between you. Continue to pass each other six to eight times, moving closer each time, until you are close enough to allow the dogs to sniff each other. Praise Rover for the appropriate behavior that he exhibits toward Spike every time he approaches or is near the pup. Distract him with a toy or food if he appears to be upset over the pup; DO NOT give him any food treats, though, if he is growling at the pup; he will be receiving a reward for the wrong behavior! Giving Rover a *collar correction* could cause him to dislike the pup; on the other hand, it could settle him down. (Collar correction—quick jerk of the leash to tighten the collar and then instantly releasing the tension on the collar. It helps to break the dog's concentration and warns him to pay attention to the person holding the leash.) You need to know ahead of time what will work better with Rover—treats, distraction, or collar correction—so that you can inform the person handling him how to deal with any inappropriate behavior. Next find a place to sit where the dogs will be about six to twelve feet apart and cannot reach each other. Once both dogs have settled down and ignored each other, you should observe Rover. Is he calm, or is he rigid? Is he quiet, or is he muttering? If he is calm and quiet, you can let go of the leashes, put a hand on both of the dogs, and pet them.

Watch the dogs; pull Rover off and away if you see any signs of aggression toward the pup. However, do not confuse discipline with aggression. If the pup is being pushy and in Rover's face, it is natural for the older dog to put the pup in its place by growling and lunging toward him and possibly even pinning him. A dog who is relaxed with the pup and then growls at it, grabs him by the scruff of the neck, and physically places him against the ground is just pinning the pup and disciplining him. Yelling at the older dog would be enough, usually, to make him back off and let go of Spike. Once the dogs appear to be okay with each other, take them home in separate vehicles, as Rover may be possessive of the car.

At home, take them both out to the backyard and observe their actions. Before bringing the pup into the house, be sure to pick up all of Rover's toy. If Spike has a chance to play with the other dog's toys without Rover around, Spike may think the toys belong to him. Then when Rover disciplines Spike for having a toy, poor Spike won't understand the reason why.

When it's time to bring the pup into the house, leave the older dog outside. Spike needs to have the opportunity to explore his new home without the older dog becoming protective over any particular spot. Without toys around, Rover may not be so possessive over the house. When you bring out any of Rover's toys, bring out the ones he likes least. This way he won't be so apt to discipline Spike for having one of his toys. Also, put the toy out on the floor instead of giving the toy to the pup. If Rover sees you giving Spike a toy first, he may decide that Spike needs to be taught a lesson about the proper ranking order. Usually an older dog will get along with a younger one for quite a few months before deciding to teach ranking order to the younger dog.

If, after the initial introductions, the older dog stays tense— his tail raised and stiff, his body and face tense or tight, he trembles or growls/rumbles constantly—you'll need to take extra measures. (Aggression toward the puppy would result in an all out attack on the pup that would not end until you intervened by physically restraining the older dog.) Keep the dogs apart until you have read the following two chapters: "Multiple Dogs" and "Bringing Home Baby". Some dogs will take at least a few weeks to accept the pup. For others, you may have to seek help from a qualified behaviorist.

If you have a cat or other kinds of animals, it would be better to put them into a room and shut the door when Spike first comes home. Once Spike has become accustomed to his new home, put him on a leash and let out the cat. Do not allow him to chase the cat. If he does, he'll have discovered a way to get the house into an uproar and will not stop chasing the cat until the cat really swats him. For any other animals, such as guinea pigs or ferrets, walk Spike up to the cages and allow him to sniff and observe the animals. After a few minutes, take him away and distract him from the other animals by playing with him. If you allow Spike too much time to observe the other animals, he may think that you want him to jump in with them and start playing, except his play will be too rough for the other animals. Try to play games with Spike while the cat or other animals are out. If Spike gets more attention when the other animals are out and less attention when they go into their cages, he'll actually look forward to having the other animals around. (This is the same way to teach a dog about a new baby.) The more often they are out and about, the more attention Spike receives. When the animals are not in the same room as Spike, he receives less attention. It's the quickest and best way of teaching Spike how to get along with other animals.

The First Night

The first night will probably be a little rough on both the pup and you. He'll be missing the warm cuddly bodies of his littermates and may do some crying and fussing. Giving him attention at this time will teach him to fuss to get you to come to him. Now is the time to give him the toy or towel that you brought back from his first home. Because it has the smells that he is familiar with, it will help calm him. Sometimes a warm water bottle wrapped up in a towel will provide him with one of the warm shapes that he got used to when sleeping with his brothers and sisters. Then again, some pups will chew on the water bottle and end up sleeping in a puddle. (*Do not* put an electric heating pad in with the pup. If he chews on the cord, he could certainly end up in serious trouble or even dead!) And finally, adding an old ticking wind-up clock (also wrapped up) will simulate the heartbeats of his siblings and thus provide him with comfort.

If his crate is in the bedroom and you hear him fussing, wait until he is quiet for a few seconds. Then get up and take him out to the bathroom. This way, you can shorten the time it will take to house-train him. An average size Labrador retriever pup at eight weeks of age has a bladder the size of a walnut—not a lot of room for holding all that water he drank during the day when he was nervous. Just think how much smaller the bladder is on puppies of smaller breeds and how much more often they will need to go out.

The Next Few Days

Take time to choose the right name for your dog. Do not name him something that rhymes with common commands (e.g., "Sit," "Stay," "Heel," or "Down.") The name you give your puppy will actually be a separate command—a command for attention. When you call your puppy's name and he looks at you, praise him.

Be sure that when you name your puppy, you'll still like the name and feel it suits him even when he's being obnoxious, when he's older, or when you are talking to someone else about him. Names like Sweetums, Pooh Bear, and Baby can be embarrassing to owners when the dogs are no longer puppies. However, using a nickname when you are talking to someone about Spike will keep Spike alert and ready for action when he hears his real name. For instance, if you use his real name when you are on the phone with a friend or have a friend over—and don't need Spike at that moment in time—you are actually teaching him to IGNORE his name. Also, you may use his name to let him know you are happy with him and use a nickname to talk about Spike when you are displeased with him. Nicknames are fun for the family to think up and can be quite inventive.

Work on rules for the whole family to follow with the pup. Go over rules, responsibilities, and duties for all of you and the dog. Be sure that everyone follows the rules. The puppy will settle into his new home faster if everyone treats him the same and disciplines him the same way.

Who will be Spike's main caretaker? Usually this falls to the adult who is home the most, but everyone should help. Some of the children (if they are old enough) can take turns feeding the dog, letting him out, and supervising him. They can check daily that the dog has plenty of clean, fresh water and also help brush him and train him. Getting a dog for the kids and expecting them to take total care of the animal is *very* unrealistic! Children can and should have some responsibilities in connection with the dog, but only with adult supervision (*children* refers to the age group of four to twelve). ***Never*** assume that a child has remembered to care for the dog—always double check.

Will he have freedom to roam the house? For a puppy, this is not wise, even if you are in the house. If you can't see him, almost guaranteed, he is getting into or doing something he shouldn't. It is not easy to house-train a puppy who keeps leaving accidents in rooms where you can't see him; by the time you do get to him, it's too late to correct him. It is wise, for at least the first few months, that you do not allow Spike freedom to roam unless he is supervised. Having a puppy or young dog in the house is like having a toddler; you need to childproof your home.

Leaving Spike loose in the house unsupervised is another way of telling him it is okay to steal food off the counters, clothes out of the laundry basket, play with shoes, and so on. The best cure for stealing is prevention. Leaving a pup or young dog alone for any length of time, not crated, is a potential problem no matter how well you have dog proofed your house. He can still chew the furniture or electric cords.

Is the pup going to be allowed on the furniture? If not, don't pick him up and put him there as a small pup. Start the pup off with the restrictions you want to impose on him when he is full grown. It is easier to give more freedom (allow him into more rooms in the house, more time out of the crate, etc.) as the pup gains maturity and listens to commands better. It is much harder to enforce restricted areas and keep him off the furniture if you allowed it to happen when you first brought the puppy home. If you want to let your puppy get on the furniture for some snuggling and petting, give him permission to do so by having him do something to earn the right. And make sure he gets off when told. But never let Spike do anything that you don't want him to do when he is grown.

Consistency is very important in training a puppy or a dog. Commands should be given in the same way by everyone, and everyone should deal with unacceptable behavior in the same way. When dogs get mixed messages, they learn much more slowly— or not at all. Children should be allowed to help train the puppy only with adult supervision! Children nagging or pulling on the pup can result in Spike learning to ignore the child, knocking the child down to get away from him, or nipping or biting the child.

Sometimes, cuddling with your pup or dog on the floor makes Spike think he can be more mouthy or try to take advantage of the situation and walk all over you or sit on you. If you want Spike in your lap, put him there. When Spike is nine months of age and not listening to you well, one of his tricks will be to get into your lap when HE wants to. This is his way of saying "I win." Just stand up (if you can) and dump Spike off. If he is too heavy, let him drag a leash around and have another family member come by and snag him off your lap. If you're home by yourself, don't allow him to get in your lap in the first place.

Where will the dog eat his meals? Dogs can be very protective of their food dish, so it would be wise to feed him away from the major traffic flow of the people in the house. He should always be fed in the same spot. Do not move him from corner to corner or room to room as this can cause him to be nervous about his meals. Feeding him from the table can result in a dog that tries to steal food. Also, if he begs and gets fed, he has taught you to feed him when he wants to be fed. Some foods do not agree with a dog's digestive system and can cause diarrhea or, worse, problems that can be lifelong.

The best method to teach him to allow people to approach his food dish without him feeling protective is to talk softly to him as you approach and slowly reach down and add a few really good treats to his dish. As he gets used to this, in a week or so, pick the dish up a few inches off the floor and add a few really special treats to the dish and set it down again. Once he is comfortable with that, pick the dish up, set it on the counter, add a few real tasty treats, and then set it back down. The next step is to have others in the family, but one at a time, do each stage of getting him used to people handling his food dish. This way, after everyone in the family has done it (if by yourself, get friends and children over ten years of age to help you), he will expect even a toddler, older child, or stranger who approaches his dish to only add to his meal, not try to take it away.

Will the family be allowed to feed him from the table? That is not a great idea because it will encourage him to beg or steal if he feels he is not getting goodies fast enough. Some dogs even nip their owners if they feel they are not getting enough handouts. If you decide the dog should not be around the table during meal times, make sure he has a place of his own to go to, either a crate or dog bed. That way when he's told to leave the room, he'll have a place to go to.

Teach the children to allow Spike some time by himself. Every person AND animal needs some private time to just "be." Everyone in the family should respect this of each other and the dog. Even if he's lying on the floor chewing a toy, he may not want company right then. Remember the saying "Let sleeping dogs lie." Even the most placid animal will sometimes grab hold of a person when it has been startled.

Naps

Puppies that are not allowed to have a nap time, are constantly walked too far, and have "busy" hands on them a lot can be made into hyper, mouthy pups. They are also using up nutrients meant to help them grow—build bone and muscle, a good hair coat, and so on. Slow, calm hands help settle down a pup. Not getting enough naps overloads their circuits with too much stimulus.

Encourage a pup to take a nap even if you need to put him in a crate. Or put his leash on him, and stand on the leash while you settle down to watch TV or read (this is also how you teach a pup to "settle"). These naps should last for at least fifteen minutes or longer, depending on how old the pup is and his breed. You will see a difference in how long Spike will play before taking a nap from week to week. The longer Spike plays, the longer the nap will be, until he stops his fast growth phase (at about 6 months of age). Then he will play longer and nap for a shorter time.

During nap times, Spike may start growling, yelping, or whimpering, moving his legs, twitching, and so on. These are all signs of his having a dream. To touch Spike to wake him up may end up with a very startled dog. *IF* you feel the need to wake Spike up during this phase of sleep, do so by talking to him, not by touching him. Think back to one of your dreams, either good or bad. How would you react if someone physically shoved you to interrupt that dream? Your heart might race faster, you might be more upset, you might take a swing at that person (as you are not fully awake yet) or you might accept it without any problems. Spike is the same way—except in his case, instead of taking a swing at you if you startle him out of his sleep by touching him, he may snap at you. This could start a serious problem. Spike should not learn to wake up snapping at anyone who approaches his bed, brushes up against him, or walks with a heavy tread and wakes him up.

Spike and Children

A pup views a child as a littermate. The more the child plays rough, the more the puppy bites. It is his only way to retaliate. If another puppy played too roughly with your puppy, he would cry out loudly and might even bite the other pup. Then both would take it easy for a while. Do not allow children to play unsupervised with a puppy. One of two things will happen if you do: The pup will try to dominate the child, or the child will rough up the pup and make him afraid of children. As they both grow older, they can be the best of friends, but they must respect each other first.

Do you greet Spike or the children first? Granted, no one greets us as enthusiastically as our dogs. However, if you greet the dog first before greeting a person or child, you have just elevated Spike in the pecking order. He is just below you and above the rest of the family, another reason to pick on the children and to ignore any other adult.

Do not discipline Spike for growling! A growl is your warning that something is not right at that moment of time and place with the dog and whatever or whoever is around him. If you discipline the dog for growling, he will learn to bite without warning.

If you have left a room with the dog and child in it and hear growling, return immediately and separate both the dog and child. Sometimes children tease a dog past his tolerance without understanding the consequences. That is why you need to be in the room when a puppy or dog is there with a child. This way, the child can be taught by you when enough is enough. Otherwise, the dog will teach the child, and the only way possible for him to do so is by biting.

Unless a child can make a dog mind him on the first command, he should never try to interfere with the dog. Toddlers especially are targets for puppies and dogs to chase, as they move fast, wave their arms, and have high squeaky voices—a living, breathing, moving squeaky toy!

Have Spike learn that the child is his boss by having your child help feed Spike. Have the child tell Spike to "Sit," and when he does, have the child put down the food dish. With you by the child's side, Spike will usually comply. But the fact that the food is coming from the child will encourage Spike to view him not as a littermate but as a leader.

This is all *management,* not training. Management is defining boundaries for the puppy, house-proofing for potential hazards, setting feeding and house-training schedules, being consistent with what is a "No" and what the dog IS allowed to do, and exercising the dog so that he is tired and not inclined to get into trouble.

Training is teaching the dog commands and how you expect him to behave. Training is a way to communicate with your dog through command words, body postures, and hand signals. No matter how much training a ten-month-old dog has been given, no matter how well he responds to commands and is obedient, it is NOT good management to expect that dog to stay loose in the house alone for eight hours and not do some damage! Even one hour might be too long for some dogs. Would you allow a two-year-old child to be home unsupervised and in a room by himself/herself? Of course not. Nor should you consider leaving Spike home alone and loose in the house, until he is mature mentally to handle that responsibility and behaves himself. Most dogs under fifteen months of age are mentally as old as a two-year-old child, with some breeds being even slower to mature mentally.

Next Few Nights

Now that you have had a night with Spike, where will the dog sleep? Dogs are "pack oriented," so they prefer sleeping in someone's bedroom. If left in the basement or another room, they will usually whine or bark even more than if they were allowed in your bedroom. Either put a crate in your room or get him a dog bed. He will usually settle in quite rapidly to your schedule and become part of the family faster if allowed to sleep in someone's room. (You may need to use earplugs for the first few nights.) Sleeping in someone's room does not mean on someone's bed. That, in the dog's mind, would make the dog an instant equal to the human. Thus, he wouldn't need to listen and respond to anything you said or wanted him to do.

If you feel you absolutely must have the dog on the bed, make him respond to a command such as "Sit," "Down," or "Shake Hands," on the FIRST command. (Even an eight-week-old puppy can be taught to sit within a few days to a week.) His reward is to get on the bed. He must also get off immediately when told. If he does not do it on the first command, wait about five minutes and try again. If you keep saying the command, you are teaching the dog to wait until HE wants to respond to your command. This puts him in charge. If you have to pull him off, he has made you react to what he is doing and is still in charge. However, if you toss a treat or toy on the floor to move him off the bed or furniture—if you stay put and he does the work of getting himself off—in his eyes, you are in charge.

What will he sleep on? Giving the puppy an expensive wicker basket and pillow before he has finished teething just gives him something else to chew on. Letting him have an old stuffed chair or couch in the basement might rebound with him thinking that he can chew up and shred the good couch. Letting him sleep on an old towel is okay UNLESS he chews on it. Then you must take it away from him or you might be facing an expensive vet bill when he has to operate and remove part of the towel that Spike could not pass through his intestines. If he chews, he loses the bed until he is trustworthy.

You can change Spike's sleeping quarters during the first few nights. Trying to change where Spike sleeps after the first week home will be met with some resistance from him. It can be done, but you may end up with a few more sleepless nights. Really put some thought into where Spike is to sleep, and try to keep it that way. He will settle into the family faster and easier if you do.

Remember, it is much easier to start off with rules for the family and for Spike than to try and impose rules and restrictions after you have had Spike for a few months and do not like the type of dog he is becoming. While it takes time to go over the rules with the family in the beginning, it will take a lot longer to retrain the family and Spike later on. The biggest key is to be consistent and to remember that every time you interact with Spike, he is learning something—who is stronger, who backs away first, who gives out more treats, who yells loudly now but not always, and so on. Spike might as well learn the right habits and rules from the start. He will learn them faster and remember them better than if you allow him to acquire some bad habits (e.g., jumping up on people and stealing from the counter) and then try to retrain him.

Days Off

On weekends or other days off, Spike needs to be taught that you want him to remain quiet instead of getting up at the usual time. On these occasions, take Spike out at his regular time, but put him back in his crate with a pacifier to encourage him to keep quiet so that you may go back to sleep or just relax before starting the day. Perhaps a Kong toy or any toy that has a hollow end may help keep him quiet. When peanut butter or squeeze cheese is put in the cavity, the pup has to work to lick it out; this can keep him occupied for a long time! A favorite stuffed toy also may be appropriate; however, each time you give it to Spike, check to make sure that he has not opened any of the seams. You don't want him to chew and swallow the stuffing.

Gradually Spike will come to understand about weekends or days off. Unfortunately, it will take several months; so be patient.

Walking Spike and Introducing Him to Other Dogs

As a pup, Spike needs to go for several short walks a day rather than a long one once a day. Several walks a day will help tire him out more often, give him a chance to get over something that frightened him during the previous walk, and help build his confidence about going outside. When taking Spike for his first few walks around the neighborhood, take along his favorite toy. If he becomes startled or frightened of anything, bring it out and start playing with him. If you feed him a treat when he is upset, you'll be rewarding his scared behavior. A toy serves as a distraction, not a reward.

Do not be in a hurry to walk Spike around your neighborhood or a public area if it is frequented by many dogs. Spike needs to be socialized to older dogs, BUT he needs to have it done in a positive manner, one at a time, with dogs that are friendly toward smaller/younger dogs. Taking Spike to the park or beach where many dogs run together, in an established pecking order or pack will only set him up to be frightened as he will be charged by the pack. The leader may pin Spike, in which case, several others will attempt it too. Spike will assume that all other dogs are bullies and as he grows older will want to defend himself by going after them first.

When walking Spike on a leash and you see another dog, DO NOT stop walking. If you stop, the dog takes control of the situation. If the other dog acts or looks aggressive, it is better to turn toward Spike and go back. If the other dog manages to get close enough to sniff Spike, you MUST let this happen. Trying to keep Spike moving will only make the other dog more curious and determined to check out Spike, sometimes to the point of grabbing him. DO NOT pick up a puppy/small dog if another dog is approaching. This action will draw the dog's attention to you, and he may go after you to get what he wants, which is Spike! Stand your ground with Spike between your feet and in a stern voice tell the other dog to "Go home!"

Normal greeting behavior between a puppy and a dog will usually take place in one of two ways:

1. Older dog approaches pup in a normal walking rhythm. Pup lowers his body a little as the adult dog gets closer. Pup lowers head when adult dog goes to sniff him. Adult dog goes to the rear of the pup and sniffs his private areas, then comes back and sniffs noses with the pup, sniffs pup's head, and keeps his head by pup's head. Pup at that point will usually lick older dog's muzzle in a gesture of submission. Adult dog may play with pup or walk off and ignore pup.

2. Adult dog charges toward pup. This is the one where you place yourself over Spike and tell the other dog to "Beat it!" Watch and see if the adult dog slows up and approaches Spike with more care. If so, you may allow them to meet. If not, stand your ground and discourage the other dog from checking out Spike.

If you have a puppy of a small breed, be extra vigilant that he does not get run over by a bigger dog or puppy. It only takes one such experience for that pup to decide that he is either going to run away from the situation as fast as he can OR try and attack the bigger dog or pup.

While it may seem funny to watch a small breed like the Yorkshire terrier try to take on a Great Dane, even the most mild mannered of dogs will eventually get tired of having this smaller dog try to bite and lunge at him. Once the bigger dog picks up the smaller dog, it only takes a few shakes of his head to break its neck or back or to in other ways severely damage the smaller dog. Not all dogs of smaller breeds try to take on bigger dogs like this, usually only ones who have been roughed up by larger dogs.

Even a large, pushy puppy of thirty pounds may be too much for a smaller Spike to feel comfortable with at first. Interrupt any play that seems too rough. If you take the older pup off to the side, does Spike come charging back at him? If so, they can continue to play, as Spike was not that upset with the rough play. Still, keep an eye on the play in case Spike wants to end it and the other pup is not ready to do so. If Spike runs off or does not approach the older pup when that pup is pulled away from Spike, then Spike is ready for a break from playing. Spike needs to be able to escape the other pup and come back out to play when he is ready. Provide Spike with something to hide under like furniture or shrubs, and resist the urge to interface. If you keep sheltering Spike or picking him up, he will not learn how to properly play and cope with other animals on his own.

Normal greeting behavior between two older dogs or pups will have both of them going for the other one's rear end with tails raised and sniffing. Then they will turn and sniff noses and check out each other's faces. One dog will lower his head or turn it to one side and lower his tail. This is the more submissive dog. The other dog becomes the more dominant one and will then put his head over the other dog's shoulders. If that is okay with that dog, they will be okay loose with each other. If that is not okay with the other dog, he will whirl and try to put his head over the other dog's shoulders. They will settle the issue with some growls, showing of teeth, and maybe a lunge or two toward each other. This will usually be the end of it if one of the dogs is not that dominant. If both dogs are very dominant, they may fight. Break it up by making loud noises, laughing, or walking away. If the dogs have lost their audience, some will stop right away. By no means are you to reach in and grab a dog! That is the quickest way to get bit, as the dog will think another dog is attacking him from the rear. He will turn and bite without realizing he is going for a human until it is too late.

If your friend Bob has a pup and suggests that Spike and the pup get together for a play session, be sure to supervise it. When taking Spike to a friend's house (who has a dog) make sure the dog is outside when Spike first comes in the house, so Spike has a chance to explore before meeting the other dog.

Give Spike a few days to adjust to his new home before introducing him to your friend Jane's dog. Limit playmates to one dog until Spike is comfortable with that dog. Then introduce him one on one to a new dog. When Spike is at ease around that dog also, then you can have all three play together. Always make sure Spike has places to escape to if he feels overwhelmed. Spike does need to interact with other dogs of various ages to learn proper social skills. Just take it slow and easy in the beginning so that he learns good behavior and habits rather than bad ones. Remember, if Spike comes back for more play when the other dog is pulled off of him, Spike is okay with more play. If Spike seems to say "Thank goodness you came to my rescue," then end the playtime. In the beginning, it is better for other dogs or pups to come to Spike's home. He will gain confidence faster. Once he does, then he should go to Jane's and Bob's houses for visits.

When taking Spike to visit Jane's dog, she may want to put her dog outside until Spike is in the house. Some dogs are very possessive of another dog coming into their home when they are in it. Yet, when put outside and allowed back in to find a dog there, they lose that initial greeting frenzy that would have taken place. There may still be a few noises, but if Jane will speak firmly to her dog to let him know this is the way she wants it to be, he will usually back off and relax. Always praise the appropriate behavior, and you can't go too far wrong.

Now that Spike has a few doggy friends, set up a walk with Bob and Jane and their dogs. This way Spike will meet dogs while on his walk and have good experiences. He may not recognize the other dog right off, so he'll go into the proper social greeting of being submissive or at least docile, to be sniffed and examined by the other dog. Try to have some distance between Bob and Jane so that Spike has a chance to meet their dogs several times during his walk. If everyone walked around the block or within the neighborhood, Spike would have several chances to greet the other dogs both going away from his home and returning to it. Every positive experience will help build his confidence in his social skills.

Dogs will try to entice another dog, pup, or person to play by doing what is called a play bow. The dog's hind end stays up with tail wagging while the front end goes down. The dog's head will be looking at the other dog or person with mouth open and almost smiling—clearly an invitation to romp!

While all of this may seem like a lot of extra work, please remember that with most breeds of dogs, it only takes one bad experience for that dog to be afraid of other dogs, or dogs of that color and size, for the rest of his life. It is very difficult and much more time consuming trying to have Spike recover from such an experience. I know of one dog who, when brought home at 8 weeks of age, was charged at and scared by the next door neighbor's dog. The next day while out walking, two loose dogs did the same thing, and when the owner and pup got back home, the neighbor's dog came back again and this time actually grabbed and shook the pup. He is now "dog aggressive." With help, he has improved while under voice and leash control, but he is not to be trusted if loose. This is just one incident; I know of many other similar ones with the same result. Such dogs are simply afraid of being scared or hurt again and decide to strike out first—a very difficult dog to handle for a first-time dog owner!

What will you use if the other dog will not back off from Spike? You might want to carry an air horn (sold at most hardware or marine stores), a walking stick, a wiffle bat, a whistle, and so on. It should be something that will make a loud noise or that you can insert between the two dogs—something that is NOT one of your limbs! Even a pepper or mace spray will work; just make sure you aim it toward the other dog's face.

If you are home and another dog starts a fight with Spike, grab the garden hose and turn it on full blast. Aim it at the other dog; that, along with your yelling, is usually enough to discourage him.

Chapter 2

Nipping

Puppies use their mouths like babies use their hands; it is how they investigate items. A puppy cannot pick something up and feel it, so he puts it in his mouth and feels it, tastes it, and bites it. Up to the age of fourteen weeks, this is normal puppy behavior; he is trying to work out what he can put his mouth on and what he cannot. After fourteen weeks, it becomes a means of controlling the people he interacts with. He soon realizes people and especially children do not like to have him grab them with his mouth and put any pressure on their skin. Now he knows he can try to boss everyone around. Playing rough with a pup encourages him to use his mouth more. While we all want to be on the floor playing with Spike, you need to halt this type of play BEFORE he becomes mouthy (nipping, biting, grabbing), and that goes for everyone who plays with Spike.

When teaching a pup to inhibit his bite, start off like a litter-mate would if he had been grabbed too roughly. Scream "OUCH!" so loud and strong that the pup almost flattens on the floor. Do not immediately praise and pet the pup. Let him think about it for a few seconds before you tell him "Good Boy." Even if the pup grabs your clothing, shoes, or mittens, still scream. He should learn not to put his teeth on anything you are wearing, especially your skin. Young children screaming "Ouch" sound too enticing and should be closely watched when playing with a pup or young dog. This cannot be emphasized enough! Leaving children alone while they are playing with a puppy or young dog is a bite waiting to happen. Children tend to push the pup away when they have had enough, and the pup sees this as still playing. The harder the child pushes the pup away, the faster and harder Spike comes back to the child and grabs. At this point, both the child and Spike need a time-out from each other. Help your child understand that he/she needs to exercise some control over the situation and have him/her take a time-out by sitting on a chair for a few minutes. Have Spike take the time-out in his crate. If you consistently put Spike in his crate whenever he gets mouthy, he'll learn to control his actions, as he really wants to be out with his family.

When a pup grabs another pup too roughly, the pup being grabbed becomes still at first before trying to either get away or turn and go after the biter. DO NOT pull your hand, or whatever the pup is grabbing, away from him if he still has hold of it. This will encourage him to hang on even tighter! Hold still, even if he has your skin in his mouth. Use your other hand to gently cup the back of his head, and leave your hand in his mouth until he reacts by trying to spit out your hand or back away from the hand in his mouth. Wait until he strongly pushes against the hand on the back of his neck before taking your other hand out of his mouth. When he releases it, wait a few seconds and THEN say, "Good Boy."

Water pistols and/or shake cans work also to help teach the pup not to leap and grab. These take timing and DO NOT take the place of training! Rather they help enforce what you are saying, that is, "Leave it" or "No bite."

Sometimes grabbing a puppy by the scruff of the neck and lifting him off the floor when he has grabbed you or a child will get your point across in the minimum amount of time and effort. Let the puppy drop the last few inches and then totally ignore him for at least five minutes. With the wrong pup or young dog though, this could rebound and make matters worse. It is offered here as a way that some people deal with this situation and get results. Before doing any physical punishments/corrections to your puppy or dog, think about the ways it could work and the ways it could make matters worse. For instance, with a shy or insecure dog, it could certainly make matters worse.

Trying to grab Spike and wrap your hand around his mouth to close it before he can bite you is not a good way to deal with the problem. He ends up turning it into a game. Can he grab you before you grab him? You might get away with it with a very young pup for a few weeks, but then watch out, as his reflexes will be as fast if not faster than yours. If you have to withdraw your hand and then try again and again before you get his muzzle, why shouldn't he look upon this as a new game? You are not being an effective leader since it is taking you too many tries to get the message through to him.

Another way of dealing with nipping that takes timing and coordination on your part is to try and tap his lower jaw shut quickly and firmly **but** not slamming it shut. If you miss, you might hit one of his teeth and so you have hurt yourself and again not gotten the message through to the pup. While slapping his mouth shut may relieve you of some anger, it does not teach Spike anything except to be afraid of you. Not a great way to start out what could be nine to fifteen years of life together! This is included as a method that has been used before, but it is not a good way to deal with the problem. It usually creates a dog that is hand shy or aggressive.

You can always keep placing something in the pup's mouth to take attention away from you or a child. Give him what is appropriate to chew on so that he learns that it is not you. It is natural for pups to chew on anything they can put their mouth on. After sixteen weeks of age, though, it becomes a way for the pup to control the people in his family.

You should try to find ways to praise Spike for touching you and NOT grabbing you. If he licks you, tell him "Good Kiss" and that he is a good boy. With enough repetitions, Spike will learn the proper behavior; instead of nipping you, he'll lick you.

Is Spike eating three meals a day? If he is hungry, he becomes nippy faster. Does he inhale his food? If so, he doesn't think he has enough to eat. Put two large rocks in his dish. This will slow him down and he will realize he has had enough food and slow down his nipping.

Is Spike being more mouthy and nipping because he needs a nap or because you're not stopping the playtime fast enough? If Spike is able to behave himself for thirty seconds of playing before getting mouthy, then that's when you should stop playing. Gradually build up the time—even if it is second by second—that he can continue to play without getting mouthy. The best way to end playtime is to remove yourself from the area and become occupied with something else. If Spike becomes insistent that you resume playtime with him, give him a time-out in his crate.

Chapter 3

Teething

A pup starts to lose his teeth as early as three-and-a-half months of age. The canines or fang teeth come in at about six months of age along with his molars. From about five months up to nine months of age is when he'll do most of his chewing, trying to make his gums feel better.

It is during this time that Spike will go through rawhide chewies almost hourly. Other toys would be Gumabones and Roarhide bones, both made by Nylabone. These are easier to chew up than the other Nylabone products. You'll still need to be watchful that Spike does not chew off too large of a piece and try to swallow it. He NEEDS things to chew on—make sure these things do not include the couch, the kitchen table, or an electric cord.

Feeding him frozen carrots will be of some help. Being cold, they will make his gums feel better, and if the carrot is of decent size, chewing it to pieces will keep him occupied for a little while anyway. Also, letting him chew on ice cubes will be of some help.

Putting an old wet washcloth in the freezer and letting him chew and suck on that will help also. BUT make sure you are around to watch that he does not swallow it, or you could end up with a vet bill for removing it.

Between his chewing and trying to steal items, having a puppy around is one of the best ways to teach the rest of the family to pick up their belongings. Since Spike is going to chew, better that he chew on something you give him rather than on what he chooses, which is usually a piece of furniture.

If Spike has not chewed on anything that he shouldn't have and he is over nine months of age, don't think you are out of the woods yet! **EVERY** dog will chew. It's just a matter of when!

Chapter 4

House-Training

New puppies already have an instinct for house-training. Dogs are pack animals and feel very strongly about keeping their dens clean. In order to house-train your puppy, he'll have to be taught that your whole house is his den and must be kept clean. Be consistent; always use the same door to take Spike outside to go to the bathroom. Eventually, he'll tell you that he needs to go out by going to that door. Putting sleigh bells on the door and teaching Spike to hit them is one way for him to be able to tell you that he needs to go out even when you don't see him go to the door.

Puppies who have been in pet shops are the exception to keeping their den clean. Unfortunately, they have little choice but to go to the bathroom in their crate, and it usually passes through onto another floor. Puppies who were raised in an unclean environment will also be harder to house-train. Such pups can be house-trained and crate-trained, but it will take more time and effort and lots of outs to go to the bathroom.

Along with your puppy's instinct for cleanliness comes a built-in schedule of eating, sleeping, playing, and elimination. Observe your puppy's habits and use these observations in your house-training program. A feeding schedule establishes a puppy's toilet routine. Puppies eating three times a day usually do well being fed at 7 A.M., 2 P.M., and 6 P.M. Your pup is usually ready to skip the middle meal when you find that he is not eating all the food at any of the meals or that he eats two meals well but leaves some food behind at the third meal. This usually happens when the dog is around five to six months of age.

The more consistent and vigilant you and all members of your family are, the faster your puppy will be house-trained. The more you can stick to a routine of taking the pup out, the sooner he'll learn not to go in the house and will try to hold it, as he knows he'll be going out shortly. If you take him out five minutes after he eats today, don't wait thirty minutes after he eats tomorrow before taking him out. If your puppy seems difficult to house-train, you'll need more time and patience and help from the whole family. When a puppy needs to go out in the middle of your favorite TV show, he can't wait for a commercial.

Confine him to a very small area, like a dog crate, and he will let you know when he has to go out, since he won't want to soil his den. If you are not going to have Spike's crate in your bedroom, consider putting it in a room with a linoleum floor. Enclose a small space with the crate in it and line the floor with newspapers. When you are not able to watch the pup, put him in this area. Put a towel or small blanket and a stuffed toy in the crate and leave the door open. Then if Spike needs to go to the bathroom, he'll leave his crate and do it on the papers. This will train him not to go in his crate yet still confine him to a small area. Trying to house-train Spike and having him in a crate is the exception to the rule of NOT letting him out when he fusses.

He will usually fuss and make noises when he needs to go to the bathroom.

A puppy who has food left down for him at all times is more difficult to house-train. Food should not be left down for more than 10 minutes. Dawdling encourages poor house-training and does not allow you to establish a schedule. A pup eating grocery store dog food (and three meals a day) usually has between four and eight bowel movements per day! Harder to housetrain than the pup eating higher-quality food and having a bowel movement per meal and one more throughout the day. A puppy who has food available at all times usually becomes a picky eater and eats a little bit at a time. A little meal does not make him feel that he needs to go to the bathroom. Lots of little meals will catch up with him when you least expect it to. If he skips a meal for being too slow or picky, he'll be encouraged to eat better and/or faster the next time. You are the boss, and he should eat what he is given, as long as it meets all the requirements for his age.

Do not start trying other brands of dog food or cooking gourmet meals. You'll become a slave to your dog. He'll like something for a day or two and then turn his nose up at it and expect something new. After a few days of the new food, he'll tire of it and wait to see what new food you will bring home next. He is calling the shots and you are wasting money.

Pick up the water dish after 8 P.M. to make it easier for the pup to hold everything during the night. Once he is older, water should be available at all times. If he plays a lot in the evening or it is warm or hot out, he can chew on some ice cubes. This way he'll get some water but not as much as if you put the water dish back down.

Remember, puppies of smaller breeds will need to go out more often than puppies of larger breeds, as the bladders of smaller breeds are not able to hold as much. Thus, if an eight-week-old Lab puppy should go outside every thirty to forty-five minutes, an-eight-week old toy poodle should go out every twenty to thirty minutes.

Also puppies of small breeds may take more time to house-train as the average size kitchen is a huge space to them. They will need to be confined in a smaller area to help them understand house-training. They should not have access to other rooms unless you are with them.

Catching Spike in the Act

If you catch your puppy having an accident, scold him promptly by saying "Shame" or "Bad Dog," but don't use his name. Then take him immediately out to his toilet area and praise him if he finishes eliminating there. Always make the toilet area a positive place to be. A puppy will not usually become fully house-trained UNTIL he is caught in the act of going in the house! Once he understands that it is not desirable to go in the house, he'll make more of an effort to go to the door to go out. However, if Spike goes to the door in the kitchen, waits a few seconds, and then goes to the bathroom—while you are in the living room and can't see him—whose fault is that? Young pups *can't* "hold it"; the best they can do is go to the door and hope you open it.

Do not rub Spike's nose in the mess. He will not understand that action and may think you want him to eat it and clean up the area. Do not let him see you clean up the mess, or he'll think he can "go" anytime and you will be his slave and clean it up.

If you find an accident, you cannot scold Spike, even if it is still warm or you catch him leaving the room. UNLESS you see him doing it, he will not relate the scolding to the accident. You can, however, scold the accident. Call it a "Bad potty," "What a mess this is," and so on. Clean up the mess and take it outside to Spike's toilet area. Take Spike with you so that he can see where you are putting the offending material. Once he is back in the house, put Spike in his crate so that he can't see you finish cleaning up the mess.

How and What to Use to Clean Up a Mess

The most important part of cleaning up a mess is getting rid of the smell. If your dog can smell it after the mess is cleaned up, chances are that he will go in the same spot again. Most household cleaners mimic the smell of urine when they dry, so avoid using these products. (Be careful not to mix cleaners. The fumes that are given off when chemicals are mixed may be harmful.) Deodorizers made to mask the smell will eventually fade away, and Spike will be back to mess on that spot again. Dogs do this for several reasons. One, it smells like a spot they should go the bathroom on. Two, if cleaned improperly, Spike may think that another dog came into the house while he was out and marked on that spot. Now Spike has to go on that spot to mark his territory.

So, follow this procedure: Blot up the urine or pick up the bowel movement with paper towels. Take these towels outside to the dog's toilet area and leave them there for him to check on his next trip outside. In a small jar with a wide mouth, mix two-thirds white vinegar to one part water and a dash of liquid dishwashing detergent. Shake the jar and, with a slightly damp sponge or paper towel, apply only the foam to the soiled area. If the accident was done on a carpet, scrub the foam into the fibers and sprinkle baking soda onto the spot (if it really soaked down to the mat). Allow the area to dry for several hours and vacuum as you normally would. If you can still smell the urine, repeat the whole procedure. With old stains, add some of the liquid from the jar onto the stain and let it sit for a few minutes. Scrub the area, and most of the stains will disappear, along with any leftover scent. If the accident was done on a floor, clean up the mess and apply the foam to the area. Let the foam sit for a few minutes and then wipe it up.

Paper-training

Paper-training is a very controversial matter because it may be very confusing to the pup when the papers are finally removed. It also slows down the process of learning to go to the bathroom outside, as the pup first learns to go on the papers and then has to learn to go outside. Training him to go outside to begin with is usually faster and easier. In the case of very small puppies or those that will not be over twenty pounds, paper-training is done often. Also, litter box training is sometimes done with the toy and miniature breeds.

If you feel the need to paper-train, put papers in the room closest to the door Spike will be going out of. Start with the entire floor being covered in newspapers (you may want to put a plastic tarp down also). As Spike becomes consistent in going to the bathroom on certain areas of the papers, remove the rest. *Gradually,* almost inch by inch, move those papers closer to the door. The last step is to put the papers outside in the toilet area and have Spike go on them out there. Always reward for the correct responses he makes toward being house-trained!

Outside Toilet Area

It's best if your puppy's backyard play and toilet areas are separate. If he is allowed to consider his toilet area as part of his playground, it will take him longer and longer to do his duties, as he thinks he is out there to play. He should be encouraged to "go potty" as soon as he goes out.

Do not tie your puppy out to do his bathroom duties because there will be no one there to praise him when he goes. Take him to his toilet area on a leash each time so that you can give him lots of praise when he goes. This will encourage him to go quickly, and you will learn his schedule faster by going out with him. Puppies left alone to go to the bathroom think they are out there to play and will come inside the house and have an accident almost immediately. If you don't stay out with your puppy and help him focus on what he's out there for, it will take much longer to house-train him.

Take your new puppy out when he wakes up from a nap, finishes eating or playing, or starts circling and sniffing. The average fifteen-pound eight week-old puppy needs to go out almost every half hour. The fewer mistakes he makes in the house, the faster he trains. Small breed puppies usually take longer to house-train, as their bladders are so small and even the smallest room is so big to them. As the puppy gets even a few weeks older, he can *gradually* go longer and longer between the times he needs to go out. It is not fair for even a mature dog to be expected to hold it for more than eight hours, even if he can. If he is not totally house-trained by six months of age, you need to re-evaluate your training. Or maybe Spike has a urinary-tract infection. Take a urine sample to the veterinarian to find out.

Doggy Doors

If you have other dogs and have a doggy door, Spike will soon learn to go out through the door. But, unless you go outside with him, he will not learn to become house-trained! It is too easy for Spike to follow the other dog outside and come back in the house without ever going to the bathroom. He needs you to go outside with him and praise him when he goes to the bathroom outside.

Once Spike understands about housetraining, a doggy door is a super way to allow him free access when he needs it to the outside, as long as the backyard is fenced in!

Teaching Spike How to Let You Know He Has to Go Out

Do not expect your puppy to tell you when he needs to go out. Most pups do not go to the door; rather they start sniffing and walking in small circles. This is their cue to you that they need to go out. If you are fortunate enough to have a pup go to the door, you need to be very observant and make sure the pup goes outside **every** time he goes to the door! This is one way to teach a pup to let you know he needs to go outside. Saying "Do you need to go outside?" will also become a cue to him. You can hang sleigh bells from the door and teach the pup to hit them with either his nose or a paw. As soon as the bells make noise, you open the door and take the pup out. When the pup becomes bored though, he may run over and hit the bells so that he has someone to pay attention to him.

You can also teach him to go to the door and bark to go out. Praise him for spontaneous barking by saying "Speak" right after he barks and giving him a reward. After quite a few repetitions of this, try asking him to "Speak." If he does, give him a big reward. If he does not, he needs to hear the word more to associate it with what he is doing. Once he will speak on command, take him to the door and ask him to do so. When he speaks, open the door and take him outside. Again, when he becomes bored, he may go to the door and bark so that he can be let outside. Then he may bark to come back inside—and do this repeatedly. Thus, he's learned another way to get attention. To avoid this problem, once you know that he has done what he needs to do outside, any further hitting of the sleigh bells or barking should get him no attention, or even a time-out in his crate.

Suggested Schedule of "Going Out"

Try this schedule:

- Take Spike out first thing in the morning . . . (with a young pup, that means even before *you* go to the bathroom, if he is awake).
- Take him out after each meal . . . (within five to ten minutes).
- He should go out after each nap . . . (even if the phone rings, the kettle boils, the best part of the movie is coming up, etc.).
- And he should go out after each play period . . . (and sometimes *during* a play period, if he stops playing and starts looking around).
- Finally, don't forget to take him out last thing at night . . . (if you go to bed early, you may want to set your alarm clock to get him up and out during the night—until he is a few months old).

Most pups regress and start making a few more mistakes for anywhere from one to five days before finally learning to be house-trained. Hang in there. Puppies are not house-trained overnight. But then, neither were you!

Chapter 5

Submissive Urination

Giving ANY attention to a pup when it submissively urinates only makes matters worse. There are a number of reasons why some pups (and some adult dogs) do this. Some pups are on the shy/quiet side. They may be intimidated by someone in the family and feel the need to slink or crawl when that person looks at them or walks toward them. Or they may sit but be almost cringing. If you pat this pup while he is acting like this, you are rewarding the behavior. Over time, the dog will try to please you by becoming even more submissive, and urinating when approached is a sign of being the most submissive he can be. In a pack of dogs, that is a big way of saying, "I am not worthy; please don't beat up on me; I know I am the weakest member here; I'm scared of you." This is NOT how you want your dog to greet you. If anyone else were to observe this action they would think that you beat your dog. Only greet this type of dog when he/she is not acting submissive, otherwise you will just reinforce the incorrect behavior.

No matter why the pup is like this, the way to deal with it is the same:

1. When you come in the door, do not make eye contact with Spike and gently toss him either a toy or a treat. Try to aim the object just ahead of Spike and off to one side so that he changes direction slightly to go to it.

2. Go sit down and ignore Spike. If he comes to check you out, put out a hand, BUT do not look at him.

3. Allow no one to pat Spike if he lies on his side. This encourages the submissive behavior. Spike only gets attention when he is standing or sitting. Use high-test treats (e.g., cheese or meat) or a favorite toy to encourage Spike to hold still and accept attention. Trying to physically hold and support him will only lengthen the time it takes for Spike to overcome his insecurities.

4. Avoid making sudden movements the first few minutes of coming into the house. Make sure all family members and/or visitors do the same.

5. Take Spike for walks in populated areas. At first, take him to areas that do not have a lot of people. As he becomes calmer in those situations, take him to areas where there are more people. Eventually, he will realize that he is not the focus of attention and will overcome his being so submissive. Do not let anyone pat Spike if he

flops on his side. This will only encourage him to continue to be submissive outside of the house. He should sit for people to be able to greet him. Take along a favorite toy or treat to help him stay focused on sitting and to ignore the people.

Do not let Spike see you clean up any accidents. Usually it is the first five minutes that are the most crucial with Spike and any submissive urination. Ignoring him as much as possible once you have tossed the distraction will help also. With you and everyone else following the above steps, eventually Spike will overcome this behavior. DO NOT assume that Spike will outgrow this! If Spike is nine months of age or older and you are still having problems, seek help from a behaviorist.

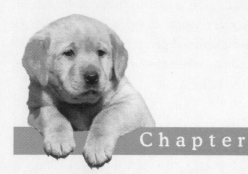

Crate-Training

Why a Crate Is a Good Idea

Before going any further, call up your mother, aunt, and grand-mother and ask whether they ever put their babies in a playpen. If they say yes, ask them why they used a playpen. (Bear in mind that some people never believed in them and called them an evil invention that allowed a mother to be away from her children.) Take a few minutes and think about having a toddler who won't nap. How will you take a shower, or finish a cup of tea or coffee before it grows cold, or have a few minutes to yourself? Those are all valid reasons for keeping a baby safe and secure while the parent has time for himself or herself. The same reasons apply for using a crate—to give the dog a way to escape from the family, to have a den where Spike feels secure and safe, or to give the owner a breather from making sure that Spike has not put something else in his mouth. Or where will you put Spike if you break a glass? Can you quickly put him outside or will he run loose out there? If he is a thin coated dog like a Doberman or a Greyhound and it is winter out in the northern part of the United States, Spike will not be able to stay outside for long. As you can see, a crate is closer to hand than shoving Spike outside while you take care of the mess.

If you have not thought of using a crate to put Spike in while you are away, please think about it for a moment. Where is he going to stay while you go to the store, to work, or out to dinner? What damage can he do with his teeth while you're gone? If you want an excuse to replace the sofa or kitchen table, by all means leave the pup in the same room with it; you'll almost certainly be guaranteed that sooner or later the pup will try to eat it.

What if he pulls over a lamp or chews on an electric cord? He could get cut from the broken lamp or severely shocked or even killed from biting an electric cord. Almost anyone who has a child has used a playpen. The crate is for the same purpose. When you are not around to supervise the pup or dog, you can put him in the crate. You can put him in the crate if you need a time-out from watching him too. However, just remember that if the pup is in the crate too much while someone is home, he is not learning how to get along with the family or learning his manners and commands. Instead he is learning to be independent **from** the family and, unfortunately, will not bond as well.

Getting Spike Used to His Crate

There are many different methods to teach Spike to go into his crate and like being there. But first you need to choose the style that is right for you, your family, and your situation. Another important consideration is where the crate should be placed. Which room and then which wall makes the most sense? How much sun will shine into the crate and possibly make Spike too warm? How much time will Spike spend in the crate each day? And what about the size of the crate?

To have Spike willingly go to his crate anytime he is told, he must form a good association with it. Use a command such as "Kennel," "House," or "Bed," so that he knows you want him to go in the crate. If he eats in it, chases his toys into it, walks by and finds an occasional dog treat in it, the crate won't seem like such a bad place.

Feed Spike in his crate so that he gets used to going into it. In the beginning, don't shut the door. He needs to feel comfortable in it before that happens. As he gets more relaxed about the crate, start shutting the door for longer and longer periods of time. Remember though, shortly after a meal, a pup will need to go out to the bathroom.

If he doesn't chew towels or blankets, he can have one in the crate. If he goes to the bathroom on it, don't give him another one until he is house-trained.

Save his favorite toy and put it in the crate when you need to leave the house for a while. This way, he gets his favorite toy and will not be so upset over being in the crate while you are gone.

Most pups will howl their first few nights away from home whether or not they are in a crate. With some pups, having the crate in the bedroom will take care of the matter. With others, you may need to use the water pistol and "squirt" them to be quiet— but first, are you sure Spike does not have to go out?! Still other pups may need to be put in the garage or basement in the crate until they get used to it. This may sound cruel, but if you are a light sleeper and Spike keeps you up four to five nights in a row, you will probably give in and bring him up on your bed, which means that Spike has learned to get his own way.

If you make a big deal over Spike coming out of his crate, he'll want to come out faster and faster each time he is in it. Treat it as an everyday boring routine thing to do.

Never let Spike out of the crate when he is barking or whining (unless you think he needs to go out and even then try to wait till he's quiet for a few seconds before letting him out), as this teaches him to whine or bark whenever he wants to get out of the crate. Either ignore him until he quiets down for at least ten seconds or make him be quiet. This can be accomplished by using a water pistol or a shake can. Water pistols that are small enough to fit in the palm of your hand are unseen by the dog. If you hide the nozzle of the gun with your first finger and trigger it with your second finger, Spike will think that your finger is shooting the water! Shake cans are empty soda or beer cans that have been rinsed out and had ten to fifteen pennies added to them; put tape across the opening so that they won't fall out. Place an old sock over the can so that the dog does not think that every soda can is meant to be shook at him. Shaking the can when Spike is intent on doing something you do not want him to do gives you a chance to get his attention. Once you have his attention, you have a chance to redirect him away from what is enticing him.

How long should Spike stay in a crate during the day while you are at work? Certainly adolescent dogs can go longer between potty breaks, but they still should not be in a crate for longer then six hours at a time. A pup should not have to spend more then an hour in a crate at a time or his chances of eliminating in the crate increase as each minute goes by. Make arrangements for someone to let Spike out if you cannot follow those time-frame guidelines.

If you are going to be gone for any length of time, consider whether you want to leave water in the crate with Spike. If he is bored, he will probably drink all of the water in the first half hour that you are gone and then need to go out to the bathroom. Then, poor Spike is home sitting with his legs crossed. Or if he is a pup, he will probably end up going to the bathroom in the crate.

If Spike is an older pup but still needs to be in a crate, consider attaching a large hamster-type water bottle to the crate. Obviously, Spike will need to be taught how to use it. Leaving a bowl that sits in a wire frame that attaches to the crate bars will work also. However, some dogs relieve their boredom by removing the bowl from the wire. Same with leaving a regular dog bowl in the crate. Spike may amuse himself by flipping it over. If you are not going to be gone long, than Spike does not need any water left in his crate.

Play music softly when leaving your pup in the crate so that he feels he is not so alone. Keep the volume turned down, as his hearing is much better then yours. Leaving the TV on once in a while will give him a change of noise.

Choosing a Crate

A crate that will be big enough for Spike to stand up in and not touch the top when he is full grown may be too big for him as a pup. If Spike goes to the bathroom in his crate and still has room to not touch it, he has learned to eliminate in his crate rather than to hold it. Sometimes you can put a divider in a wire crate to keep the pup at one end. As he grows, you can enlarge the area until he eventually has the full crate. Spike should be able to turn around in the crate easily and almost stand up straight without having his head touch the top.

A wire crate is harder to clean up (sometimes) if the pup has an accident in it. However, it does allow for more air circulation and a chance for Spike to see more of his surroundings. And it is easier to section off a large wire crate than it is to section off a fiberglass crate. Putting a piece of plywood on the top of the crate allows it to be used as an end table, a grooming table, a place to hold his collar and leash, a toy, and so on. Some pups in a wire crate may need to have an old blanket placed over it so that the crate more closely resembles a den. Most pups instinctively know about dens and feel safe and secure in such a place. If you put newspapers or an old towel under the crate pan, it won't hit the wire supports underneath it thereby possibly scaring Spike when he steps into the crate.

A fiberglass crate makes the dog feel more secure (sometimes), as it is more enclosed. It is easier (sometimes) to clean up accidents in it. Fiberglass crates usually maintain a better resale value. However, less air goes through them, and some dogs are less happy in this type of crate, as they cannot see as much around them. Be careful of buying or renting a used crate that has zinc fasteners rather than plastic one. The zinc fasteners, if swallowed, can be toxic to pets.

If you have a puppy that will grow into a large dog, you may want to consider renting a crate. Some veterinarians, boarding kennels, or obedience clubs may have crates they will rent for a small fee. This way, you can keep exchanging the crate for a bigger size as the pup grows rather than buying new ones. You may also want to check the ads at animal hospitals for crates for sale. Check the local flea markets or garage sales also. Just be sure to really clean the crate once you get it home.

As most pups will not soil the area that they sleep in, keeping Spike in a crate when you are not around to observe him will facilitate his learning to be house-trained. Just remember that he will continue to use his crate as a bathroom if he has room to not touch it.

Location of the Crate

Where is the crate going to be? Dogs do like to sleep in the bedroom with us, as they listen to our breathing and feel comforted that they are with others. But if you put it in the bedroom, you now have to go a further distance each time Spike has to go outside while he is being house-trained.

Is the crate in a drafty area of the house? Is it too near a window so that in full light, Spike will become too hot? Is it near a source of heat that would make Spike too warm and his coat dry? Is he out of the main travel path of people walking from one room to another?

Perhaps you can buy a second, used crate from a vet, boarding kennel, obedience club, or garage sale (scrub it out thoroughly with bleach and water to kill any bacteria) and put it the kitchen or family room. This way, Spike has one crate to sleep in near his family and another to stay in during the day—located near the door Spike uses to go outside to the bathroom.

Dogs like to be around people and will bond faster if allowed to do so. However, you should put their crates in a place where a lot of people are NOT going to be walking past. This allows them to have a nap and not be constantly waiting to see who will pass by next.

Sanitation and Safety

Make sure to clean any new crate (especially one that you rented or purchased used) extremely well BEFORE letting Spike go into it. You do not know the health condition of the last dog in it. A mixture of one cup of bleach to one gallon of water will kill viruses. Make sure to wear gloves on your hands and wear old clothes in case the bleach splashes. Also, do the cleaning in a well-ventilated area.

A dog should **never** have a collar on and be left in a crate when no one is home. If part of the collar gets caught in the crate and no one is home to help Spike, he will panic. The potential for severe problems occurs at this point, possibly even death.

Are children allowed to be in Spike's crate when he is not in it? Is Spike possessive about his crate? If a child likes to be in the crate and follows Spike in when he goes to lie down, will Spike bite the child? With proper coaching to both children and dog on acceptable, appropriate behavior, everyone will get along just fine. Above all else, do not let any children, either yours or those of visitors, stick their fingers into Spike's crate. This is an accident waiting to happen. Even if Spike is okay with this behavior, what if a child gets a hand or finger stuck and starts screaming? Maybe this would upset Spike enough to grab the stuck finger or hand.

After a few positive experiences, Spike will look upon his crate as a place of security. All you need is time and patience.

Chapter 7

Stages of Development

There are many stages a young dog goes through both physically and mentally. Physical growth and weight gain are more obvious. Mental growth may not be so apparent, unless you are looking for it. A pup at eight weeks of age will have all of the brain cells that he will ever have. If he was with a good breeder, he has already learned to interact with the other pups in his litter, he has already started to learn to interact with people and to like them, and he has been allowed to explore new areas to gain confidence.

Spike will start off a little leery of new experiences, objects, and sometimes even people and other animals. After every fearful phase will come the confident phase. Once he gains confidence (with his owner's help sometimes), he becomes more bold and sometimes very pushy in asserting himself. He may try to demand more attention, or more playtime, and he may be more stubborn and resistant to responding to your spoken commands.

Two to Nine Months

Between the ages of two and four months, the puppy undergoes a stage where he fears everything. This is the time to get him out to explore new environments, but do not let him be overwhelmed! Go slowly but surely. Encourage him to approach things he fears, like a fire hydrant, a garage door, or a swing set. Try to have him walk on different types of surfaces. Some studies show that this increases confidence and ability to handle situations. Even if he will be a large breed when grown up, he may still be picked up and put on an examination table at the vet's office. It is better for you to practice this with some treats at home so that Spike is comfortable with being up off the ground **before** he goes to the vet and has something done to him that he may not like. The more he broadens his horizons, the more secure and confident he will become.

The more he stays home, the more confident and protective he will be on his own turf. But when he does leave his own property, the more insecure and unsure of himself he will be—sometimes to the point of becoming aggressive, as he does not know how to behave properly. Some breeds of dogs must learn correct social skills with people and animals when they are young, or they may never learn.

Socialization and Submissiveness

Between the ages of two to four months, the pup learns how to react to his world. Some of his opinions may never change. If his way of dealing with another dog is to charge it and bite it, this will always be in the back of his mind, even with exceptionally good retraining. It is VERY important that the pup be socialized and exposed to his world in the right manner to avoid problems in the future. This includes introductions to other animals and children. Having a big black dog run at him and knock him down will teach him to dislike big, black dogs. This dislike can grow into trying to fight with any big, black dog he comes across.

A pup who flips over on his back and shows his belly is being submissive. If you pay attention to Spike when he does this, he will think this is the way you want him to greet you. While it does stop him from jumping on you, it also looks as if you beat him. Spike needs to learn to stand on his four feet to greet people, not lie on his back. Dogs that continue to be submissive in greeting learn to show the same response when reprimanded. If other factors come into play—his food bowl is left down all the time, Spike is allowed to sleep on the bed, he constantly asks for and receives attention—the dog becomes more dominant but in a sneaky way. Spike shows you how contrite he is when you turn to scold him, and as soon as your back is turned, he is back doing what he wanted to do, like steal the sandwich off the counter. These dogs usually end up going to another home, as the owner becomes tired of dealing with this type of dog. If Spike is fed at set times, is not allowed a lot of liberties, and has to earn some of the attention he asks for, then he is likely a good dog, just more submissive than he needs to be.

The way to stop submissive behavior is to ignore it. Only pay attention to Spike when he is not on his back. If you scold him and he flips over, take him out of that immediate area so that he won't try to go back and get into whatever he was in when you started to scold him.

It is extremely important to do the neighborhood introductions with care and playfulness so that Spike will not be afraid. If you keep your pup home a lot during this time period, as I said earlier, he will grow up to be very confident and secure at home but unsure of how to handle situations away from his property. In some cases, this could lead to the pup being extremely fearful and shy of people, other animals (even if he has other animals at home), and going to strange places. These fearful dogs usually end up biting due to their fear. In this day and age, it will probably mean a lawsuit and having to find new home owner's insurance. Thus, it is important to take your pup to a lot of different places and situations, but never let him be overwhelmed. Bring along his favorite toy and/or a few treats so that he has a positive experience even when he is not sure of why he's there and how he should react. If you can laugh convincingly whenever Spike becomes fearful or shy, you will help him immensely. Most dogs do not think a situation can be very harmful or bad if their owner is laughing. This is called the "Jolly Routine," and it even works well when you think two dogs may get into a fight.

Depth Perception

A puppy does not have good depth perception until about twelve to fourteen weeks of age. So use care and patience in teaching him to climb or come down a set of stairs. Some puppies have an especially difficult time with coming down the stairs. Don't just yank on his leash and force him down. Put the pup up on the second step from the bottom and encourage him to come to you while you are sitting on the floor with a toy or treats. Give him lots of praise when he does this! Then pick him up and put him on the third step from the bottom. Keep doing this one step at a time, and he will quickly learn how to come down the stairs. Getting his meal at the end of doing the stairs will be a big motivation and a great reward for doing it all on his own, with voice encouragement from you.

Attempts at Dominance and Independence

Sometime between the ages of three and nine months, Spike may try to hump your leg as a way of trying to become more dominant. DO NOT laugh at him. This will only encourage him to continue to do it to you and to try to do it to everyone else. Use a water pistol, shake can, peel him off—whatever it takes to get Spike off your leg. Try to do this as silently as you can. Once he is calm and has all four feet on the ground, you can talk to him.

By the time the pup is four to five months of age, he has become aware of the size of his backyard and his room in the house. Instead of being a shadow when he is outside with you, he will start to wander, usually into the road! He has started the process of being independent and confident. In the house, he will go off to find something to do out of your sight, usually mischief. At this stage, do not allow any new freedoms or privileges; he will see them as permission to continue going his own way.

Fearful/Shy Period

Between the ages of seven and eight months, the puppy MAY go through a fearful/shy period again. Use the same tactics that worked with Spike in the past to get him to overcome his fear or hesitation with something. He will go through this stage faster than the first one if he is handled correctly!

Talking

Also, by the time Spike is seven to eight months of age, he may start "talking." This is not growling; rather it has a different pitch and may sound more like several notes strung together rather than the single sound of a growl. A growl may sound like a rumble, *but* that sound does not go up or down so much in range of tone as talking does. This is another reason *not* to discipline for a growl; Spike may be trying to talk, and in the first stages, you may not realize it. With some dogs, it becomes very clear what sound is a growl and what sound he makes when he talks. With others, it will take longer to make that distinction, as their talking sounds more like a growl. If the dog is relaxed—no strain on his face, tail possibly wagging—he is talking. If you push or play with the dog, he may even raise his tone some more. If Spike has only one tone of voice for both growling and talking, you and the family will need to be extra careful that playtime is ended before this noise escalates and he becomes mad, with no apparent warning.

Smiling

Also at this age, he may start to smile at you, another person, or another animal. Again, look at the Spike's body language. Is he calm or tense? Is his tail wagging or stiff? Is he quiet or growling? If he is calm, quiet, and maybe the tail is wagging, he is smiling at you. He may be able to do this with both sides of his mouth, though most dogs do this with only one side of their mouths. Some dogs smile as a way to show pleasure in seeing a person or dog or even a new toy or treat.

Nine to Twelve Months

Between the ages of nine and twelve months, the puppy has become confident with his environment. By this time, he is usually house-trained and knows your schedule and his. This is the time that he tries to declare his independence; he may also become protective of his home, car, and family. In addition, it is the time that he sets for life his attitude toward people and other animals. He thinks he is ten feet tall and bullet proof. Now is the time to remind him that you are the leader. Again, don't allow any more freedoms or privileges. Work on having the dog respond to your first command. What will be the penalty or correction if he does not? This is **NOT** the time to put a prong/pinch collar on Spike! What may start out as lunging in a friendly manner toward other animals or people may turn into a dog that lunges out of aggression. In the wrong hands, a prong collar can turn into a heavy duty correction that does not fit the crime or action of the dog. Spike then decides that the person or animal is responsible for his neck suffering, so he retaliates by becoming aggressive toward them. This is difficult to overcome but can be dealt with through a concentrated effort on the part of the owner and a knowledgeable behaviorist.

Fifteen to Eighteen Months
"Deaf Attitude" and Testing Stages

Between the ages of fifteen and eighteen months, the dog undergoes a "deaf" attitude. He has hit the teenager stage and must be handled with the same amount of fairness and tact as any teenager. Being too rough physically at this age will usually result in someone getting bitten. If you have not already neutered your dog, you now may want to give it serious consideration. Being without hormones reduces the dog's "drive" to challenge your leadership.

Some individual dogs and certain breeds like the Rottweiler go through another testing stage around three years of age. Up to this age, they might have been pretty good dogs; but if they test you at this stage and win any battles, they will be set in their attitudes for the rest of their lives, always trying to be the leader and not obeying you.

Five to Seven Years

"Deaf" Attitude Again

Between the ages of five and seven years, a dog will become "deaf" again. This is another time in the dog's life when he will not listen to commands and try to do as he pleases. Some people relate it to the dog trying one last time, before he is too old, to take charge of his pack. Whatever the reason, just define the dog's boundaries better (make him respond to the first command, bring back penalties for wrong behavior, etc.), and he will usually fall back into his regular role in the family. This is also the age when a lot of spayed female dogs develop urinary incontinence and start leaking urine while they sleep. This can be easily corrected with medication. This is also the time frame where most dogs become more upset over thunderstorms. Their hearing has changed a little, and they can hear different tones. This can cause the dog to worry about his hearing and make him overreact to sounds that before did not bother him. Don't overreact yourself, and don't tell him it is okay and pat him a lot. This will actually make him more scared. Tell him to "be a big kid, be cool," and so on. Laugh at him; try to get him to play with you. Do what you can to take his mind off the approaching storm.

Thunderstorms, Stress, Anxiety, and Emergencies

There are two homeopathic remedies that work well with dogs that are scared of thunderstorms. They do not make the dog groggy like tranquilizers do. *Aconitum napellus* and phosphorus are two homeopathic remedies that can be given to a dog that is afraid of thunderstorms or fireworks, without making him sleepy. One remedy may work better for your dog while the other remedy works better for your friend's dog. Usually, if it is going to work, you will see improvement within ten minutes. The remedies are in pellet form and cannot be touched—the natural body oil on your hand will destroy their efficacy. Pour about four pellets into a small paper cup and then pour the pellets into the dog's mouth. If there is a slight improvement, you can give a few more pellets within five minutes of the first dose. This can be repeated every five minutes for a total of four doses.

The remedies come in "strengths" of either x's or c's, with c's being stronger. That does not mean that a 10-pound dog that is really afraid of thunderstorms needs a 30c remedy. A 6x will usually work well. As with human medication, more is not always better. If you see some improvement but not enough with a remedy of 6x, try a 30x remedy. If better but still not as calm as you would like to see Spike, try 6c and so on until Spike is calm and functional. If Spike is somewhat calmer but still not where you would like him to be, contact a homeopathic veterinarian for further help.

Bach Flower Remedies are useful for thunderstorms, stress, anxiety, and emergencies. The Rescue Remedy is great to give during an emergency. The other remedies can be used in combination with each other or singly. There are thirty-eight remedies in alcohol-based preparations. Due to the alcohol base, some animals do not tolerate the preparations as well as others. If you like the idea of using the Bach Flower remedies but Spike cannot tolerate the alcohol, look into dried herbs. Your local health food store will be able to help you with reading material, and they may know of a very knowledgeable herbalist whom you can contact. Also, if they do not carry the remedies you need, they probably can order them for you.

Senior Years

As dogs reach the senior years of their lives, some seem to start acting like puppies again. You can call it senility or whatever, but they can become destructive in the house, tearing up paper, pillows, and so on. They can even have accidents in the house. If this should happen, don't overreact; it is normal. Just realize that the muscle tone is not what it used to be, and so the animal may need to go out to the bathroom more often. It may also be their way to try and get a little more attention, or they may have some mental lapses about how well house-trained they had been. In some cases, an exam by a veterinarian and some medication may resolve the problem. In the case of being destructive, either bring the crate out again or start putting baby gates up to restrict the dog's access to rooms while you are gone. In the case of mental lapses, retrain the dog by treating him like an eight-week-old puppy that needs to be house-trained. Seriously, take the older dog out every half hour for a few days, increase to an hour for a day or two, then increase to two or more hours between trips. In a week or so, the older dog will be back on schedule.

This information about the stages of development is to alert you so that you can help Spike through the stages more easily and know when to tighten up on your leadership skills. Raising a pup is much like raising a child. They both have their angelic moments and those when you wonder if you will survive with any amount of sanity left. Use common sense as much as possible, and you will do just fine.

Remember that temperament is what Spike is born with. Training and socialization are the skills you need to teach him. And behavior is the effect of training and socialization on temperament.

Chapter 8

Fearful and/or Shy

Puppies often go through fear periods during the ages of two to four months, about seven to eight months, fifteen to eighteen months, again at twenty-two to twenty-five months of age, and some breeds, like the Rottweiler, at around 3 years of age. Some fear periods last for one incident; other fear periods last as long as a week. When Spike is fearful, he may sweat through the pads of his feet and pant more, he may be more resistant to go past certain objects on his walk, and he may be more resistant to training.

Overdoing any corrections or penalties during Spike's fear period can make him more hesitant to approach almost anything, even objects that he is not normally afraid of. If you do go overboard and then realize that Spike is in one of his fear periods, take him back to what bothered him. With distractions, treats, laughter, and time, you can make him confident again.

When a puppy does not want to go past something that at that particular moment seems scary to him, DO NOT baby him, DO NOT talk to him with baby talk or soothingly, DO NOT use a squeaky voice, DO NOT pat him slowly and calmly, DO NOT tell him it is OKAY, and DO NOT give him any food treats. All of these things tell the dog that he is right to be scared and that he should continue to be so. DO NOT drag him up to the object and force him to confront it! This will make him even more afraid of it the next time he encounters this object. DO NOT overwhelm Spike.

Instead, expose him in small, short time periods to whatever is bothering him. "Jolly" him along, tell him that he is being silly, laugh at him, try to get him to go up and investigate what is bothering him. If you can touch it with one hand and crouch down, you will be encouraging him to come near the object.

If Spike is tentative around children, having a group of children handling him all at once will be too much for him. Have one child handle Spike with slow hands and a low voice for just a few minutes. You should softly praise and pat Spike while he is being handled by the child. This will let him know that you approve of this. A high-pitched tone of voice will excite Spike too much. Wait about thirty minutes and have another child repeat this procedure. The time interval gives Spike a chance to go over the scenario in his mind and realize that he was not harmed by it. With repeated sessions like this, it will not take long for Spike to warm up to children who are sitting and being quiet. Once Spike is accustomed to these children individually, have them get together in a group and handle Spike ONLY if he comes to one of them on his own. As Spike becomes more outgoing with the children, have them start to play with each other, but they still need to stay fairly quiet and calm. Eventually, Spike will be okay with children. It may take Spike several weeks of getting together with children to overcome his insecurities. Obviously, all of this needs to be done under adult supervision. Feeding Spike a treat while he is tentative around children will reward him for that attitude! As time goes by, Spike will become more and more insecure around children, which is just the opposite of what you want.

A shy pup that greets you by immediately turning over and showing you his belly will only be encouraged to continue greeting everyone this way **IF** you return the greeting. Ignore the dog until he is up on all four feet. Even looking at the dog is a form of attention.

Regardless of Spike's age, if he ducks his head when someone is reaching to pat him, have the person pat him under his chin, or the side of his neck, or on the front of his chest. People reaching quickly for the top of his head to pat him may make Spike hand shy. Dogs that are hand shy look as if someone has abused them. In most cases, that is not so. Pups are instinctively apprehensive of anything coming too fast over the top of their head.

With dogs that are shy or fearful of people, have a friend help. Pick someone who will follow your directions without improvising on his/her own—this is very important! Put some treats in the room where you and your friend will be sitting. Have Spike on a leash, let your friend in the house, and ask him/her to have a seat. You sit down about six feet away from your friend with the leash under your fanny or under your foot. Spike should only have enough slack to lie down, not to go and visit OR to run away. Talk to your friend and totally ignore Spike. After Spike has settled down and seems to be calm with the situation, usually about fifteen to thirty minutes, give your friend a treat, something special that Spike does not usually get. Ask Spike if he would like to go see your friend. Have your friend hold the treat in the palm of his/her hand, with the hand being beside the person, not held out away from the body. The friend is to totally ignore Spike, no talking, no touching, not even eye contact. You should ignore Spike and the fact that he took a treat from another person. Act as if this is normal for him. After Spike has eaten the treat, let him walk around. If he comes back to your friend, he/she can offer another treat—but again, no talking, touching, or eye contact. Tell Spike that this is a "Friend." Use that word whenever Spike meets someone you want him to be friendly to. Once Spike gets used to the word and that friend, have another friend come in and do the same routine. Build success one "Friend" at a time, and pretty soon Spike has lots of friends and is no longer fearful of most people. (Dogs do not have to like everyone they meet anymore than we do.)

Some pups/dogs will submissively urinate whenever someone comes into the house. Trying to correct the dog will only make matters worse. Leave a toy or treat outside for the company to bring in with them. As soon as the visitor comes into the house, he/she should toss the item a few feet off to the side and not toward Spike. The visitor should not make any eye contact or talk to Spike. Have the visitor sit down and ignore Spike. After repeated visits from friends, Spike will become more confident that he is not the center of attention and will be calmer about being greeted. The submissive urination will disappear. Most friends who like dogs will usually greet the dog first and you second. This puts Spike at the top of the ranking order in his mind and causes conflicts within himself. At home, without guests, he knows the proper ranking order, but then company comes and disrupts it, and he does not want to be top dog and greeted first. By ignoring Spike, you allow him to relax and be himself around company.

Don't be impatient with a shy or fearful pup/dog. You will only make matters worse and lengthen the training time. If you feel yourself getting upset, it is better to walk away and take a break instead of making the dog confront his fear at that moment.

Encourage the shy/fearful pup to play tug of war with you. Let him "win" the object more often than you do. This will build his confidence.

If the vacuum cleaner is one of the frightening objects to Spike, try to introduce him to it by playing with him around the machine when it is turned off. Feed him in one room and have someone else turn it on and off in another room. Leave it out in the middle of the floor and play with him around the machine. Encourage him to chase something around it or retrieve a toy past it. Once he is comfortable with it off, turn it on—but do not move it! If you do this daily, in a few days Spike will not be so upset to see you pick up the wand, turn on the machine, and move it. If Spike does run away, put the wand down and laugh at him.

If the pup won't approach the cleaner, pick him up and carry him over to it. Sit on the floor with him in your lap and touch the vacuum. When introducing any new or frightening object, always speak in a soft, firm, funny tone of voice (but NOT baby talk). Try to jolly him out of his fear. Never chase the puppy with the vacuum, or he may never learn to be comfortable around noisy household appliances. This "jolly" routine should also be used whenever Spike comes across something that he is startled or frightened of (e.g., balloons, sounds, animals, and objects).

Dogs that are afraid of the car or get carsick a lot should be fed in the car (without it moving). Once the dog readily goes into the car to eat, drive the car to the end of the driveway (no matter how short) and back, shut the car off, and feed the dog. Keep *gradually* lengthening the ride. Get to the point you can drive about a half mile, take the dog for a short walk or playtime, put him back in the car, drive home, and give him a small amount of food to eat in the car (you do not want to feed him a full meal, as he has just exercised, and it may make him vomit or have other problems). Once you change the dog's outlook on the car—it takes him to places where he can have fun and stretch his legs—he will get better about getting into the car and won't be so car-sick. Using a human medication called Bonine may help Spike. You can usually find it in the drugstore next to the Dramamine. It works much the same as Dramamine but without the drowsiness. Using the homeopathic remedies mentioned earlier (for fear of thunderstorms) may help also, as they deal with the dog's fright itself, not what he is actually afraid of.

While the fearful or shy dog may take more patience and effort in the beginning, he can be turned into a super dog with lots of self-confidence and ease around people and other animals. Anything worthwhile takes time. The more time you invest, the better the dog.

Chapter 9

Training and Shaping

Good communication is the key to understanding and relating to anyone, human or animal. To have a working, loving, harmonious relationship between you and your dog, you must first understand how your dog sees you. Do not allow him to help himself to the popcorn that fell out of the bowl and onto the coffee table today and then punish him when he does the same thing the next time you have popcorn. Consistency is the key to any type of training. But remember the *PRAISE*! Without praise there isn't any reason for your puppy/dog to try to please you. Being praised is Spike's paycheck. Would you work for someone else for no pay?

But in some instances, being too consistent will have Spike trying to manipulate you! If you always take Spike for a walk at 8 A.M., he will try to make you take him out earlier for that walk. Same with feeding him at a set time. He will try to advance that time so that you end up feeding him earlier. If he is making too much of a pest of himself, put him in the crate. Once you give in to his urgings, you are under his control.

You should be consistent with rules and boundaries. What is allowed, and what is not allowed? Spike will learn faster once these rules and boundaries are in place.

Dogs can understand us better than we think. They read our body language to know how to react to a situation. The dog bought for a guard dog that turns into a lap dog does so because of your body language and how he sees you as a leader. (This does not mean that in order to be the boss and have him mind you, you have to beat him.)

Your posture and attitude will convey your true feelings to your dog, even if your words are saying something else. To be convincing when scolding, look and act angry so that there is no doubt about what you mean. Also, keep any scolding short in duration! It should be to the point and done with. Animals do not carry grudges for hours on end. When you praise, put your heart into it! Let your dog know you are really pleased. This will encourage him to try and please you more often. Try getting down on the floor to talk to him at his own level. This will let him know that you are friendly and happy. Try not to use baby talk or excessive petting when he is scared of something; it reinforces his sense of insecurity and makes it harder for him to accept the situation.

You are your dog's primary role model; it is your job to take the time and responsibility to educate your dog. If you are frightened of an object, Spike will become frightened of it also. If you start a game, Spike will play with you. If you are hyper, make fast hand motions, and pat the dog briskly, you will cause him to be more active. If you want to relax, teach him to settle down by your side and just hang out with you until you are ready to interact with each other again.

Building a Relationship

Every time you interact with your dog, he is learning something. If you are not teaching him the right behavior, he is learning the wrong behavior. Treats will entice him to do the commands, but once the treats are gone, he will not obey you. You can force the dog to do what you want if he is within reach, but when he is not, how will you enforce the command? Being a leader helps, as dogs understand about having a leader that the rest of the dogs follow. Being a benevolent leader is the best—firm, fair, consistent, and fun to be with. Being a good leader will only strengthen a relationship with your dog.

No training can begin until you have a relationship with your dog. If you do not have a bond/relationship with your dog, he will not learn as fast because he does not feel the need to please you. Some dogs may need to be hand fed to understand how important their owners are to them. Without a human around, how do they get fed? Trying to do hand feeding with a puppy is counterproductive. The puppy is in a hurry to be fed, and he has no clue what gets him the food. Some pups need to be over six months of age to do hand feeding. If you do not have a good relationship with a younger puppy, you need to ask yourself why. Puppies will bond usually quite rapidly to those people who spend time interacting with them.

With hand feeding, Spike must go to the owner, who has the food, and, nugget by nugget, get the food ONLY when he makes eye contact with the owner. If the dog looks away too many times during a feeding, the dog should lose the right to any more food until the next meal. He needs to learn that his owner is his reason for staying alive. If Spike nips at the hand or grabs the food and gets some skin too, he needs to be taught to take food gently from a person.

To teach Spike (at any age) how to take food gently, first let him take a treat off your open palm. If he lunges for it, close your hand over the treat so that all he sees is the back of your hand or fist. Do not take your hand away, as he will try to go after it with more determination. When Spike is calm, open up your hand and try again. If he takes it nicely, tell him "Good Gentle" and praise him some more. As he becomes better at taking a treat gently the first time it is offered to him, tell him to "Be Gentle" just BEFORE he takes the treat. If he darts or lunges for the treat any time, just close your hand again over the treat. Once he understands the concept of taking the treat gently from your open palm, try offering him a treat while holding it between a thumb and finger. In the beginning, use low-test treats (e.g., pieces of his dry dog food, and crackers). When he understands the concept better, use high-test treats (e.g., cheese and meat). If you use treats that smell enticing in the beginning, he will be more inclined to lunge for them. This lesson needs to be taught from the moment you offer Spike his first treat. If you let Spike lunge forward and grab the treat from you over and over again, for months on end, you may have to resort to a more physical means of teaching him to control himself.

You need to try several ways to find out what works for you AND Spike. Some people tap Spike's nose with a finger of the hand NOT holding the treat, just before he makes contact with the food and after being told to be gentle. This may make some dogs hand shy or devious—that is, he may try to figure out how to get the treat and avoid the finger.

Some people tap on Spike's chin with their free hand, just before he touches the treat and after being told to take the food gently. While this may not make him as hand shy, as might the first physical solution, it also may cause him to become sly.

Other people put a cotton work glove on the hand holding the treat, and just before Spike touches the treat, they tell him to be gentle. If he grabs the treat, the hand is shoved into his mouth and withdrawn, and Spike does not get the treat. After a few repetitions of this, most dogs will back off; however, others will become MUCH worse. These methods are here as suggestions. They do not ALWAYS work on EVERY dog in EVERY situation. Every dog and every relationship between a dog and his owner is different. What may work with one dog may not work with another dog, even of the same breed. You need to do what feels right for you and Spike. Depending on the dog, I have used all of these methods over time. Closing your hand is the simplest and best solution. However, when dealing with dogs who do not have good manners and are much older and forceful, a more physical method may work better. ALWAYS start with the easiest and best way of dealing with a problem before going on to something physical.

Puppies need to be taught to walk on a leash and to accept the leash. When the pup has been home a few days and is comfortable with his collar, it is time to introduce him to the leash. Attach a four-foot piece of light line to his collar and let Spike drag it around the house for a few minutes at a time. Keep a close eye on him so that he does not get the end of the leash wrapped around anything and give himself a correction. With some puppies, this type of "correction" is all it takes for them to be afraid of having a leash attached to their collars. With puppies of small breeds, you may need to use a short piece of venetian blind cord. Once he is okay with the leash in the house, take him outside.

Let him drag it outside; you follow after him. Once in a while, pick up the leash and follow him. Don't let the leash pull tight but don't run after him if he is running. You will scare him. Drop the leash instead and pick it back up when he is walking. Keep the sessions short and positive. If he becomes at all fearful of the situation, DO NOT use baby talk and pat him a lot. Laugh at him, call him a silly pup, and use a squeaky toy or treats to get him back to his positive attitude.

After a few days like this, pick up the end of the leash and encourage Spike to follow you. Pat your leg, use a toy or treat, but DO NOT drag him! Even if he only follows you a few feet, the two of you were successful; so end the session on a positive note. Try it again twenty to thirty minutes later, if possible. Eventually, he will walk with you and not have a problem being on the leash.

Dogs that have fenced in backyards sometimes resent the leash as they are rarely on one. At some time in that dog's life, though, he will need to be on a leash (e.g., to go to the veterinarian, boarding kennel, or groomer). Wouldn't it be nice not to have to struggle with Spike to get him there?

Walking with Spike is a way for both of you to get exercise and a chance to do more bonding; it is also a matter of trust. If he does not have a good relationship with you, why walk with you? On the other hand, can he trust you not to jerk on the leash and cause him pain?

A walk in which Spike pulls you all the time is not fun. It's a chore! Try to look upon the walk as a way for you to be away from the house, phone, kids, and so on, while you are out with Spike. This is your time to regroup and maybe put those thoughts together or make plans. If Spike pulls you, why are you walking with him? If he pulls and you continue to walk with him, he is learning to walk with you in that manner, out ahead and dragging you—not the most pleasant walk but certainly a fast one! There are many ways of stopping Spike from pulling. However, the following method makes a lot of sense to him. When Spike pulls on the leash, stop dead still. It's simple and easy to do; just stand still. When he slackens the tension on the leash, even if it is by turning his head to look back at you to see why you are not moving, start walking again. As he begins to understand this concept, wait for more and more slack to appear in the leash before moving again. Spike is being taught to take some of the responsibility for his walk in a way that you don't end up with tennis elbow from so many collar corrections. With this method, you will also be able to teach Spike to walk "off leash" in a SAFE area. Just stand still when he gets too far away from you. In the beginning, that should only be a few feet—anything further and he is too far to be able to keep with you if he should see something he wants to go after.

What if Spike has had enough of walking and sits down? What if he hooks one of his front legs over the leash? Or what if he simply lies down on his side? How are you going to get him back to walking again? Well, if you are strong enough, you can keep on walking and drag Spike until he gets to his feet and then praise him; you can give him collar corrections until he finally reaches your side and than praise him; you can wait him out— once he is on his feet again, head for home; or on the next walk, you can put a more forceful collar on Spike. Are any of these scenarios a way to keep a good trusting relationship with Spike? **NO!** The following is the best solution to Spike's inertia:

Take a few minutes and encourage him. He may be frightened of something—in which case, jerking on the leash will only increase this fear. Instead, next time you get ready to go for a walk, bring along a lure for Spike. Take a squeaky toy, a Kong toy with cream cheese or Cheese Whiz in it, or whatever toy will work in luring Spike along when he puts the brakes on. It may take a few more minutes during the walk to entice Spike, but in the end, he will look forward to going for a walk with you rather than dread it.

One method people use to have Spike walk nicely involves jerking on the leash whenever he pulls you. Have you ever tried handing someone one end of a rope while you are holding the other end and have that person give it a good tug? What is your instant reaction? Is it to pull back? That is the same way Spike feels when he is given a tug.

Don't forget that he has two more legs than you do and that he is very inquisitive, independent, and/or protective. Does he really need to heel right beside you for miles and be miserable because he can't sniff the ground, slow down, or speed up?

Putting a training (choke) collar or prong (pinch) collar on Spike may make him more responsive in the beginning, but you are still telling him when to behave rather than teaching him to be responsible and not pull. Eventually, with a choke collar, he may learn not to pull. But in the meantime, that may permanently damage a young trachea so that he will cough when pressure is applied to his throat, usually for the rest of his life. A prong collar will not cause that type of damage, but if put on a dog when he is eight to twelve months old, it may change his outlook about people and other animals—NOT for the better.

These types of collars require quickness and some force to make them work correctly. Not everyone has the coordination to use such pieces of equipment.

Standing still is something most people can do regardless of the size of their dog. And no one is left feeling bad for possibly hurting the dog or having the dog change his opinion of his owner. Another method is to spin rapidly as soon as Spike gets a little ahead of you, and some dogs consider this a great game. But some people are not able to spin rapidly without getting dizzy or falling, so why take a chance on injuring yourself?

Make walks fun for both of you. Just because you walk in the same direction each time you take Spike out does not mean that you can't be inventive during the walk. Do you have to walk in a straight line, or can you take a few steps backward suddenly? How about zigzagging across the road? Go in a large circle with Spike on the inside (this will keep Spike close to you, and you will have more control over him). If you keep Spike guessing as to how you are going to walk, you suddenly become much more interesting to him, and he will want to walk with you to try and figure you out. Remember, leaders make the choices. Be unpredictable!

While hand feeding and walking may seem like training issues (and they are to some extent), they are really about being a good leader and having a good relationship with your dog.

Shaping Behavior

When your puppy is young and just learning, try to shape him into trying to please you as often as possible. If you are constantly saying "NO!" to the pup or scolding him for doing something wrong, he will gradually stop trying to please you and wanting to be with you. Shaping a pup's behavior means you focus on the things the pup does right and praise him for it. When the pup sits, even though you did not tell him to *sit,* say, "Good Sit." This will help him understand what the word *sit* means and that he pleased you. When the pup licks you, say, "Good Kiss." This will encourage a good behavior, kissing, rather than a bad behavior, nipping.

Shaping behavior in this manner takes more initial effort and observation on the owner's part. However, the dog will be trained much more quickly this way than if you are inattentive and end up correcting him AFTER the fact for getting into something he should not have.

Shaping behavior also means being able to distract Spike just *before* he does something wrong. You can use a sudden sharp noise to distract him; for example, you can drop a book, clap your hands, or whistle. By distracting him at the key moment, you will be able to praise him for responding to you. Shaping builds a relationship. Always correcting him after the fact may make him view you as an adversary or a way of controlling you as he made you pay attention to him.

Correcting Spike after the fact will eventually train him, but it will take longer. With shaping, you would say "sit" every time Spike sat. In a short time, between the unasked for sits and the training sessions to teach the word *sit,* Spike will learn what *sit* means. In the beginning, all commands are just so many words to Spike—you might as well be speaking a foreign language.

Tell the pup "Good Quiet" when he is being quiet. It is too late to say this when he is barking. If he only hears the word *quiet* when he is barking, he may think that being told "Quiet!" means keep barking.

Positive motivation means encouraging the dog to continue doing something you like. You like it when Spike sits, so keep quietly praising him for sitting. When he gets up, stop praising. Do you like it when he retrieves something? If you only praise him when he is next to you with the object, he will think being next to you (or in front of you) is what you like. However, in reality, it is the whole process—Spike leaving you to go to the object, picking it up, and returning to you. He should be encouraged the whole way through, with more enthusiastic praise when he is next to you.

If you are not sure whether you want your puppy to continue a behavior or action, think about him doing it six months from now or a year or two years from now. If you want the action to continue, think of what you will call/name it and wait for it to happen again. With enough repetitions and positive responses, it will become a command.

One way to extinguish an undesirable behavior is to teach Spike to perform it on command. For example, if you do not like the pup to paw you, name the action and keep saying whatever that word is until Spike does it on command. Once he will do it every time you ask him to, slowly ask for him to paw you less and less, *gradually* over a period of a month or so, until you finally stop asking him to paw you. This is one way to extinguish a behavior. With this method, you must be very consistent in asking for the behavior every time it happens and then asking for it less and less once the dog knows the command word.

If you try to stop a behavior you do not like by constantly scolding or punishing the dog, you will actually take more time and effort to always be Johnny-on-the-spot to discipline the dog for doing what you did not like. Remember, with this method you are always reacting to what the dog just did, not interfering and changing the outcome. Scolding or punishing Spike after the action for something you did not want him to do may teach him what you want but more slowly. He is getting attention from you for incorrect behavior which is better than being ignored.

By shaping and using positive motivation, you have taught Spike better behaviors—kissing instead of nipping, trading for stealing—that you can praise him for. And because he did it on command, you can extinguish a behavior by not asking for it anymore.

Training

Puppies learn by playing games. If you make learning fun, you will train the pup more often, and he will learn faster. If you start a game with the pup and end it when YOU want to by taking the toy away and putting it out of reach, you are in charge. He who is in control of the games IS THE BOSS.

Try to work with the puppy/dog as often during the day as possible. There should not be any set time for training. If you set aside fifteen minutes twice a day to train Spike, he will think those are the only times during a day that he needs to listen to you. When you want to train Spike, take a few moments and think about a few items. Did Spike just have a meal? If so, he won't be very hungry and willing to work for a treat, no matter how enticing it is. Is he due to have a meal in a little while? If so, he may be too hungry to focus on what you are trying to teach him; he will be in a hurry to just get the treat. Is he due for a nap? If so, just trying to keep him alert and entertained will require more effort on your part.

Puppies/dogs when first learning anything need to be taught in thirty to forty-five-second increments throughout the day. Staying on one command too long bores the dog, and each repetition will get slightly worse than the response before. End while you are ahead, with the response you want! Drilling away on the same command will cause Spike to think that you really were not pleased with his response; he will try to change part of how he does the command to see if he pleases you better the next time.

Whether you train with or without food or with or without petting, if you do not praise, there is no reason for the puppy/dog to try to please you by responding to your commands or signals. Praise, petting, and treats are all the pup's paycheck. Would you work without pay? Why should Spike?

Remember, any attention, even negative attention, is better in Spike's mind then no attention at all. If Spike can do something wrong and get attention, he will continue to do it just so that you will pay attention to him. A good example of this is when Spike jumps on you. To get him off, you look at him, you talk to him, and you may even yell at him. Maybe you try to push him off. All of these things give Spike ATTENTION!

What should you do? IGNORE Spike. You should not even make any eye contact—until he gives you the behavior you want, with all four of his feet on the floor. NOW you can give him some quiet praise and attention for doing what is right.

To get this behavior, you may need to walk past him with your arms folded across your chest, eyes straight ahead—go change your clothes, put on the tea kettle, or make a phone call—until he gives you calm, quiet, all-four-feet-on-the-floor behavior.

What shouldn't you do? You may have heard of kneeing a dog in the chest to control jumping. This action has the potential hazard of rupturing his diaphragm and collapsing a lung or both. Holding his front feet and trying to step on his back feet may result in your breaking one or more of his toes. (Sometimes the dog unbalances the person, who falls over backward. So now the person has potential for injury.) You could hold his front feet up until he wants down, but is everyone else capable and willing to do this to teach Spike not to jump?

Who is in charge when Spike is allowed to greet visitors first? Put him on a leash and make him settle by your side until he is no longer interested in the company, however long this takes. Once he is lying down and relaxed, you can let go of the leash and ignore him. If he gets up and jumps on the guests, pick up the leash and bring him back beside you. Put your foot on the leash and ignore him again.

Take a step back from any situation and ask yourself, "Who is in charge of this?" Find a way that you are in charge *without* confronting the dog. If you confront the dog, some dogs will react by biting; it is their only way of telling you that you need to back off and rethink the situation.

Another way the pup takes control of a situation and gets attention is when he steals something. Anytime you chase the dog to get something away from him, he is playing a game with you, and *he is in charge.*

One way to remain in control is to teach the dog the word TRADE. Start by trading the dog a piece of cheese for the toy he is chewing on. He must release the toy to accept the cheese. Tell him "Trade, Good Boy." When he drops the item, take it away and hide it. In a few minutes when he's not looking, put the item back down on the floor. Do this fairly often throughout each day. Always tell him "Trade" before giving him a treat and taking away his toy. (You need to allow him some time to chew or play with his toy without him always thinking that you will be after it.) The next time he takes something he shouldn't, he'll come and show you that he has it. Now you're in charge as he has to admit that he stole to be able to TRADE. Yes, you are rewarding Spike for stealing, but you will be able to get objects away from him faster and more safely.

If you PRAISE Spike for trading, he respects you and sees you as a gentle leader. If you punish him for stealing, he will not show you what he has in his mouth. Rather, he will take it into another room and start chewing on it, and the item he has may not be safe for him. Remember, patience and consistency are key items in shaping.

Spike will get to the point where he will want to trade twenty to forty times a day. He is trying to fix it in his mind that *trade* always means TRADE. The one time you get tired of it and say "NO" will be the time he decides to make your paperback novel into twenty short stories. Once he is sure that *trade* ALWAYS means trade, he will quickly decrease the frequency of trying to trade.

The exception will occur when Spike is bored; then he will find objects to trade to get attention. If you keep Spike well exercised in both body and mind, he will not need to seek extra attention from you. Then you get to have a break, relax, enjoy that book or movie—as Spike is content to lounge on the floor chewing on a toy he can have.

You may choose not to use a command for this. Instead, always praise Spike when he picks something up and encourage him to bring it to you. Eventually, Spike can be encouraged to pick up anything you point to. If you want a retrieving dog, either method will help train the dog to retrieve with a positive attitude. If you are constantly scolding the pup for picking something up, don't be surprised if he does not like to retrieve when he is older.

Whatever method you use FIRST to mean "Good Dog" becomes your primary reinforcer. If you give your dog a treat for a correct response, that becomes his primary reinforcer. If you want to eventually wean him off the treats, it will not be easy and will take quite a bit of time. If you verbally praise first, pet second, and treat third, you can wean him off the food easier, as it is not the most powerful form of praise.

Treats for training should be small, something Spike can almost swallow without chewing. Milk-bone treats slow down Spike because he has to chew and swallow; thus you loose training momentum. Save the high-test treats for class or working on special projects. Around the house, Spike can work for pieces of his dry dog food, popcorn, carrot pieces, string cheese, Cheerios, and microwaved hot dogs. (Cut the hot dogs lengthwise, then cut each length into narrow sections. Place the sections between two pieces of paper towel and microwave them on high for about $1^3/_4$ to two minutes per hot dog. Caution: Large pieces of hot dog have been known to get stuck in the dog's stomach—necessitating surgery.) It is not the size of the treat that counts. The fact that Spike got a treat is the reward. To wean him off treats, do not use a variety of treats and use boring treats such as Cheerios, carrot sticks, and popcorn.

To be able to always get consistent results using treats as a training aid, make sure to vary the food offered; once the dog has learned the command, **do not** give food every time. By giving treats randomly, you will actually build Spike's desire to continue to work for you.

Some puppies need more than just verbal praise; others get TOO excited with hands-on praise. Observe your puppy to see which kind of praise, or perhaps whether a combination of both, will get your message across the best.

When teaching a new command or getting the dog used to anything—children, the vacuum cleaner, a cap pistol, a baby stroller—it is better to divide the training into stages. The second stage should take the training one step beyond the first stage, the third stage should be a small improvement over the second stage, and so on until the dog is *completely* comfortable and knowledgeable with the situation and/or the command. To rush the training or try to take shortcuts will result in confusion for the dog and his not being as reliable as you wanted him to be.

Perhaps Spike is scared of a baby stroller. Borrow one, if you don't have one, and just leave it in the family room, out of the way. Ignore both the stroller and Spike and watch him. Whenever he goes up to sniff it, quietly praise him.

The second step would be to play with Spike and *gradually* play closer and closer to the stroller. A good tug-of-war will usually have him too involved with the game to notice where he is. Fetching a toy is good also if Spike loves to fetch. Eventually roll the toy closer and closer to the stroller—always with quiet praise.

The third step would be to feed Spike near the stroller. He has learned that it won't jump out and bite him, so he probably will feel comfortable enough to eat near it.

The fourth step would be to encourage him to be near the stroller, moving it slightly, rewarding him with his favorite treats or toys. Always reward the behavior you want to continue. Don't feed Spike or give him a toy for jumping away from the stroller. These steps are only examples; depending on what motivates Spike the most, you can rearrange the order. The biggest factor is to do it slowly and *only* progress to the next step when the first one is done successfully!

Dogs get bored easily so stop after only one or two tries of the same command. If you have Spike "Sit" four to five times in a row, each successive repetitive performance will only get worse, not better! It is better to end on the first response if it was a good one, then to try and repeat it three more times. If you get upset or angry over Spike's responses, end the exercise before he loses respect for you. End it with an exercise you know Spike knows how to do well so that you still retain control of the situation.

Try to reserve the command "Come" for the times you want Spike to come to you quickly, with no sniffing or stopping along the way. You can use "Here" or "Come Here" to have Spike come to you, but he can sniff while he moves toward you. Say "Here" when you want Spike to come to you so that you can give him a bath, do his toenails, or groom him. If he does not respond the first time to "Here," it is not as important as if he did not respond the first time to "Come." Use "Inside" to have Spike come into the house, into his kennel, and so on. If you do not teach Spike to "Come" on the first command, he has learned that it is his choice as to when he responds. This will not save his life when he bolts out the front door and is heading for the road while a car is coming. Save that command for the important times, the times when you need to get him away from something potentially dangerous.

Having a puppy or dog reliably come when called takes a major training effort on the owner's part. Spike will not automatically assume that because you feed him, you must be obeyed. Think about it from his point of view: I'm free, so why should I return to you until I'm ready? There is **NEVER** a correction given to Spike when he finally does return to you! This will only make him stay away from you longer the next time he is free.

Start teaching the "Come" command in the house; with Spike close by, encourage him to come to you. Make funny noises, crouch down, be different—he'll come quickly. Give him lots of praise and maybe a treat, a toy, or a game. Success will build success. Each time that you are successful in calling Spike to you, he will store that for future reference in his memory bank. If you call him to you and can't make it happen, that also gets stored. How inventive are you willing to become to have Spike come to you rather than RUN AWAY when he gets loose? This is probably the most important command you can teach Spike; there are some training centers that offer classes just on this one subject.

Obedience Classes

Start obedience training with an organization or club that does group training. In a group situation, your dog will learn to mind you even in the distracting presence of other dogs. Once he learns to listen to you there, you have set the stage for him to listen to you elsewhere about other things—like manners or unexpected situations.

It is important to choose a training organization that deals with the dogs and owners in a manner you are comfortable with. Call as many organizations as you can in your area or fairly close by to see if you can drop in and watch classes already in progress before signing. Sometimes a class an hour away will be better for you and your dog than one nearby. You won't know unless you check out the classes.

Some classes use "clicker" training. While using a clicker may speed up the training/learning process of the dog, if applied at the wrong time, you will most certainly slow it down. Do you want to depend on a clicker to be able to work with your dog? To teach tricks or fine tune a command, a clicker is a super training aid. But it is not necessary to use it for all training, unless you want to.

If you have a puppy, pay particular attention to how play-time is handled in the class. If it is a free-for-all for five to ten minutes, a shy pup will be overwhelmed. This can cause the pup to grow up to be afraid of certain size, or colors, of dogs. He could be so afraid that he bites those types of dogs whenever they come near him. If your pup is one of the more outgoing and bold ones, then he will learn to dominate and pick on the shyer, less confident ones. Eventually, this pup can grow up trying to take on every dog he encounters. Even puppy classes that have good supervised playtime may not be right for your puppy if they have playtime every class. This practice may teach your puppy that it is more fun to **leave** you than it is to be **with** you.

Whether you train Spike by yourself or go to classes, try to remember that he has the mentality of a two-year-old child. While that child might behave in one room of the house, he/she needs to be taught that the same correct behavior is desired in all parts of the house, in other people's homes, and out in public. Spike is the same. He may know how to sit in the family room, but when asked to sit in the kitchen or dining room, he may not understand what is wanted of him. This is not Spike being stubborn; rather some dogs are not able to generalize and understand that the same behavior is okay or even expected in other locations. This dog needs to be taught sit in all locations, home and outside. Once he understands a simple command like "Sit," the other commands will be understood by him a little easier and faster, but they all will still need to be retaught to Spike in different locations.

Spike will only learn key words in the beginning. After he has heard words like *car, treat, dinner,* and so on, repeatedly, he will start to understand some of the rest of the sentences. The only difference between Spike and Lassie, Rin Tin Tin, Benji, and other TV dogs is that their trainers have words and hand signals for everything, including eating, drinking, turn left, turn right, upstairs, and downstairs.

Though it has already been mentioned, it bears repeating: *Consistency* is the key to all of Spike's training. If you repeat a command ten times before Spike does it, you are only 10 percent consistent, thereby making him only 10 percent reliable. If you repeat a command word five times before Spike does it, you and Spike are batting 50 percent. If Spike responds to your command word on the first try, he is 90 percent reliable, and you are 90 percent consistent (since neither you nor Spike are robots, 100 percent is not attainable at all times by either of you). Which percentage would you prefer when you go out together in public, or when Spike gets away from you, or when company comes to the house?

Timing is another key to successful dog training. If you praise Spike twenty seconds after he sits, he will not connect the praise with the action. The same is true if you scold or correct Spike twenty seconds after he does something inappropriate. All praise or punishment *MUST* take place within five seconds for Spike to understand it is connected to what he just did.

Management and Leadership

Teaching a dog to obey commands is a good way to communicate with him, but management and leadership mean as much in raising a pup right as any training. In fact, all the training in the world does NOT take the place of MANAGEMENT!

Management is setting rules that are consistent, giving the dog proper exercise, dogproofing the house, not allowing him to run wild in the house, but teaching him to settle down instead.

Leadership involves how Spike views you. Are you the leader or is he? Who makes the choices, who goes through doorways first, who eats first, who decides where Spike sleeps, who can take a toy away from whom? If you have answered "Spike" to any of these questions, Spike is the leader. Why should he listen to you when you tell him to do something? Why should he not have behavior problems due to the conflict in his mind as to the role he is supposed to be in within your home? He needs to take you seriously as a leader—but remember, leadership doesn't need to mean "cold."

It is unrealistic for a ten-month-old dog to be left alone loose in the house for eight hours no matter how much training he has had. Training cannot be a substitute for management. A dog that has never been to dog classes can still be a great dog if he has been managed properly.

Unintentional Training

Beware of unintentional training. Spike retains it better than regular training because the behavior is reinforced every time it happens, even if you are not home. Here are some examples:

You come home from work, and as soon as you step into the house, you see the garbage all over the floor. You know it had to be Spike, so you shout and mutter at him as he comes to greet you and continue to do so the whole time you clean up the mess. The next day it happens again. You get mad again and continue to do so while cleaning the mess up. The third day you come home and find a mess and see Spike peeking around the corner of the farthest doorway. You think he looks and acts guilty, and thus, assume that he must know that he has done wrong and that, therefore, it is ok to punish him. **WRONG!** From Spike's point of view, you have come home in a bad mood the last three days and he is checking to see if it is okay for him to come out and greet you as he used to when you came home in a good mood! His behavior has *nothing* to do with the trash unless he *just* got into the trash.

Another example of unintentional training could happen while you are out walking Spike. Say someone who is timid around dogs is walking down the street, sees Spike approaching, and crosses over to the other side of the road. In the beginning, Spike may be curious as to why the person walked so far away from him, but after this happens a few more times, he may start to sense their fear. He may now turn into a guard dog and begin barking and lunging forward to try to get the person to cross the street faster. It has become a game with him that over time will feed his ego and turn him into a bully type of dog with everyone he meets.

Still another example of unintentional training involves the mail carrier. Every time he/she walks up to the front of your house, Spike barks. Think about what happens next—the person goes away. Thus, Spike is unintentionally taught that he is a great watchdog. Spike thinks *he* scared away the mail carrier, and he can't wait to do it again tomorrow. What a great watchdog he is. Is it any wonder that Spike may try to get out the door and chase the mail carrier for not leaving his property fast enough?

Unintentional training can make Spike into the type of dog you DO NOT want to own. Therefore, it is important to watch ALL interactions with Spike so that he gets the right message about how to behave.

No matter how positive you are with Spike, there will be times when a penalty is required. There are certain times in Spike's life when he is more apt to test your authority. These times are usually between seven to nine months of age, fifteen to eighteen months, thirty-two to thirty-six months of age, and again between five to seven years of age. The type of penalty will depend on Spike—whether he is a sensitive dog, a feisty one, a dominant one, or an outgoing clown-type of dog who doesn't want to do what you want him to do right now (in other words, a dog that is conveniently deaf or defiant).

Any behavior problems that arise need to be dealt with quickly; they will not get resolved on their own and will only get worse. Going to an obedience instructor is usually the first step; however, although teaching the dog to obey commands is one way to establish some form of leadership, it is not the total answer for a number of problems. Consulting with a behaviorist, while possibly expensive, will save you money and aggravation in the end because you will be able to resolve the problem more quickly. Not all behaviorists use the same approach for the same problems. You may need to consult with more than one before the problem is resolved.

If the advice does not make sense to you, you will probably not follow it. Make sure you understand the reasoning behind the advice being given. And regardless of how good the advice is, **NO** behavior problem will be resolved without time and effort on the owner's part. There are no instant or overnight cures. As I've stated before, temperament plays a large role. It is what the pup was born with; training and socialization are skills you teach him. Behavior is the effect of training and socialization on temperament.

Speaking of temperament, are *you* in a good mood? If so, now is a good time to train Spike. If you are in a not-so-pleasant frame of mind, it will only get worse when Spike senses you are not yourself and tries to avoid being trained or does something wrong. Are you tired? Are you treating the training session as something that has to be done—so just do it and get it over with? Spike will pick up on your feelings and act out. Remember, EVERY TIME you interact with Spike, he is learning something. Make it a good experience for both of you.

Chapter 10

Penalties and/or Corrections

Spike will make mistakes; it's part of learning. How you handle the mistakes will result in how your relationship will be with your dog. To ignore too many mistakes could lead to Spike developing some bad habits that will take longer and more effort on your part to correct. To be too harsh will destroy your relationship if you have a dog who would do better with firm, verbal corrections or even having you turn you back on him and walk away.

You do NOT have to react to everything that Spike does, unless it is potentially dangerous. Take a step back and think for a moment. How do you want to handle the situation if it arises again? What will be your form of punishment or correction? If you are observant, you may be able to interrupt Spike either verbally or by dropping something before he starts his wrongdoing. Then you will be able to praise rather than of punish him. If you are not that observant or do not have much time alone with

Spike, you may end up reacting to things Spike does and never getting a chance to interrupt him so that you can praise the correct behavior. If you have to correct Spike more than five times for the same problem, you need to change how you are correcting him. He may be interpreting your correction as a reward. If you find it necessary to tether him to you, use a cord of about six feet or so. Or make sure that when Spike is out of his crate, he has your undivided attention as much as possible. Forget the book, forget the phone, and concentrate on keeping Spike out of trouble. Remember, he is much like a two-year-old child, ready to investigate anything and everything—and lecturing does not help.

Verbal Corrections

Sometimes, talking to the dog in a low, firm tone of voice that conveys just how angry you are does the trick. Sometimes total silence and ignoring the dog does wonders.

Try not to use Spike's name when you are scolding him or punishing him. You want him to like his name and to like responding to it.

"No" is heard all too often by both kids and dogs, sometimes to the point that they no longer want to try to help out or do anything new for fear they will be wrong again. Try to reserve "NO!" for times when the puppy is about to do something that is potentially harmful to him. Other times, try to use "Wrong" or "Uh-uh." Sometimes a soft spoken "No" tells the puppy that he did not respond to you correctly the first time and that you will give he another chance. An example would be that you told your dog to "Sit" (he knows this command well, usually), and he did not. With a soft spoken "No," you regain his attention and again tell him to "Sit." If he does not do so this time, he needs a penalty for not responding to your command. If you repeat any command word more then twice, the puppy is now controlling the outcome. He will mind you when **he** is ready, not when you want him to. In times of emergency, he needs to know that you mean what you say when you say it. If he is heading for the road and does not come when called the first time, he could be hit by a car and seriously injured or even killed. You don't want to have to say "Come" more than once.

Physical Corrections

Hitting the dog to get your point across only gets both of you upset and sometimes teaches the dog to retaliate the only way he knows how, by biting. Some dogs do, however, respond well to being grabbed by the scruff of the neck and given a firm, quick shake. Or grabbing the scruff of the dog's neck and pinning him (putting him down to the ground and holding him there until he relaxes and gives up) works in some cases. Some people recommend grabbing the dog on both sides of his head below the ears to make the dog look at them while they reprimand him. However, should he decide to retaliate with a bite, this directs the dog to the person's face.

Even though it is old-fashioned, taking a folded or rolled newspaper or magazine and smacking it against a table to make a loud noise can be effective. In worse case scenarios, swatting the dog across his flank with the paper will certainly get his attention. Once again, though, the dog might decide to retaliate by biting. (A bite in the hand, though, in most instances, is preferable to bite in the face.)

Being emotional when reprimanding Spike only teaches him how to get your attention when he is bored. Remember, any attention, even attention for doing something wrong, is better than being ignored. Note that any punishment by the mother dog or by the leader dog in a multiple dog household is done quickly, without emotion. The punishment is over within thirty seconds (or less), and there are no hard feelings afterward. (Animals do not carry grudges or try to get even. The punishment suits the crime. Once meted out, life goes on.)

Once you become emotional, Spike chalks up a point for himself and zero for you, as he was able to get you to lose your patience. If you already have a dog and bring a puppy home, you need to be especially careful. If you go ballistic when Rover puts his head in the wastebasket, Spike has just found a way to get you to really react when he is bored!

Remember, though, we are supposed to be the more intelligent of the species. Why get physical with an animal that can bite us?

Nonverbal and Alternative Methods

Time-outs. Some dogs respond well to fifteen-minute "time-outs" in their crates; it gives them time to cool off and think about what they did that caused them to be put there. Even though this may not be a first choice, it works great for a lot of dogs. When putting the dog in the crate for a time-out, do so in total silence. When putting the dog in the crate so that you can go out for a while, talk to him, give him a toy or a treat. He will quickly learn the difference.

Putting a dog in his crate is like sending a child to his/her room for punishment. It gets the child out of sight and out of the immediate vicinity and gives everyone time to cool down and think of how to handle the situation should it arise again. If you give Spike a time-out, he should have it in another room too, rather than in the room you are in. He needs to be the one to leave, not you, otherwise he will think he got you to leave the room, and that puts him in charge.

Silent treatment. Let Spike stay in the same room as you but totally ignore him. Do not talk to him, touch him, or make eye contact for at least fifteen minutes. With a dog who has a good relationship with his owner, this is sometimes the worst punishment you can mete out.

Water pistol. Using a palm-size water pistol has an element of surprise to it. You need to aim for Spike's mouth and/or face. If water does not bother him enough to stop the behavior, add fifty percent apple cider vinegar or fifty percent lemon juice to the water. This makes it strong enough for the dog to go "phooey" and yet not strong enough to burn the lining of his mouth or eyes.

Obviously, children should not be allowed to randomly squirt Spike. They may do so just to tease him.

Bitter Apple spray and/or cream. These can be applied to furniture, rugs, and woodwork to discourage Spike from chewing on those objects. The spray/cream may be purchased at a pet store or through a pet supply catalog. Sometimes combining the two results in an even more effective solution.

Shake cans. A shake can is an empty soda or beer can with fifteen or so pennies inside and the top taped shut. Shaking the can will get the dog's attention on you and away from whatever he is interested in.

Small, lightweight bean bags. These make a great silent training aid for suddenly getting your dog's attention (just don't leave them around for Spike to chew on!). If one lands near him and distracts him while he is barking, going for the trash, or not paying attention to you, you have an opportunity to get him to focus on you without you moving or making a noise. In cases when you must instantly change the dog's focus of attention, it will not hurt him if you hit him in the rump with a small bean bag. The dog will think a ghost hit him and whirl around looking for it. Now is your chance to have the dog focus on you.

"Booby traps." Booby traps work very well when you have a dog barking outside. If you rig up shake cans over the spot where he does most of his barking and run a lightweight line back to the house, all you have to do is be near the line and wait for the right moment to let the shake cans drop out of the sky onto him. Or if you have a dog stealing from the counter, rig up a tray of shake cans as a booby trap. Tie fishing line or lightweight cord from each corner of the tray to a centerline. Run the centerline through eye hooks on the ceiling down the hall to where you are hiding out of sight. Wait until you hear the dog's feet hit the counter and then either jiggle the line so that the cans make noise or let the line go so ALL of it falls and scares Spike. It won't hurt the dog; however, it will cause a big response to what he did. If the situation corrects him, he will remember it for a longer period of time. If you personally correct Spike for getting on the counter, you are simply teaching him to do it while you are out of the room. When you are out of sight, he will help himself.

Leadership and Control

In the canine world, there is no such thing as equals. You either lead or you follow. Who is doing the leading in your house? Letting the dog be the leader is like having a two-year-old child in charge of how you make decisions!

If you're the leader, you can prepare the dog's meal and then eat a snack before placing his bowl on the floor. Don't always have the dog do a "Sit" to get his meal; make him listen to what he is told, not what he expects to do to get what he wants! Is his food dish always left down, or is he given scheduled feedings? The dog whose food dish is left down has a reason to be more protective of his home and that area in particular. In addition, he won't know who is responsible for putting the food down. The two items that contribute to eighty percent (or more) of all behavior problems are leaving the food dish down at all times and letting the dog sleep on the bed.

Is he able to nudge you, paw at you, or stare at you to get you to pat him? Is he able to put a toy in your lap, have you toss it for him, and do this over and over? If so, he is in charge! Give him a command such as "Sit," "Down," "Roll Over." If he obeys on the first command, then his reward is some petting from you or having the toy tossed. If he does NOT obey on the first command, you ignore him. Dogs that are really being "deaf" or not complying with your commands the first time you say them need to have the control taken away from them. "No Free Lunch" is a term used by behaviorists to mean that the dog must earn the attention he asks for. These behaviorists believe that if a dog is out of control, and making decisions for himself instead of listening to his owner, the dog should have to earn attention, playtime, and meals as much as possible until the dog understands that the owner is really in control

Is he sleeping on the bed or furniture? If so, move him off by clapping your hands and encouraging him off. If he is rather large, let him drag a leash around the house when you are home; then simply grab the end of the leash, tell Spike to "Get Off," and start walking. If he does not get off on his own, he'll be moved off when you walk past the length of the leash. Grabbing a dog by his collar to drag him off the furniture is one of the fastest ways for a dominant dog to become upset with his owner and growl. Would you like someone to walk up and grab you by your shirt collar? Well neither does Spike. Remember, allowing a dog to sleep on a person's bed lets him think that he is equal to that person and, therefore, that he does not have to listen to him/her.

Also, who goes through outside doorways first? If it is the dog, he thinks he is the leader as leaders lead and the rest follow. Outside doorways and doorways into and out of the kitchen or Spike's eating area and sleeping areas are areas where the owner needs to go first through the doorway as often as possible. A workable compromise may be standing back and making the dog wait before being released to go through the doorway.

In every situation in which you are upset with the dog, think, "Who is in charge?" Was he able to make you lose your temper? If so, he is in charge. Was he able to continue doing what you did not like, even after you yelled at him? If so, he is in charge. Was he able to leave that object but go to something else just to see if he could get a rise out of you? If so, he is in charge. If it is the dog, think of how to change the dog's perception so that he sees you as being in charge. Don't be emotional when scolding; just do it and get it over with and go on with life. If he attempts to go after something else after being reprimanded, give him a time-out. Be a firm but fair leader! You will have a lot fewer behavior problems.

Holding a puppy/small dog/young dog up against you is one way of making him aware that you are being physically stronger than he, without getting into a physical confrontation. Sit in a chair or on the floor if necessary to hold the dog with his back to your chest. Keep one hand up high under his neck so that he cannot whip his head around and try to bite you. When the dog is calm and quiet, start massaging him with a few fingers on your free hand. Talk softly to him as you do this. Whenever he struggles, stop all talk and massage. When he is quiet again, gently massage each leg out to the toes and VERY gently handle each toe and toenail. This is a great opportunity to prepare the dog for having his toenails cut. With enough of this holding and massage, nail trimming should not become a major confrontation between you and your dog. Work your finger slowly and gently into each ear. This will prepare the dog to accept any ear cleaning when necessary. With puppies, gently rub a finger along their gumline to help them feel better when they are teething. It also gets the puppy prepared for having his teeth brushed.

NEVER let him down when he is struggling, or he will learn to struggle and get his own way. Start with short periods of time to hold your dog and gradually build up to a half hour each day. This gets the point across that you should be listened to without the physical confrontation of shaking or pinning. It helps tremendously with a puppy that is nipping or a dog that is dominant in his outlook toward his owner.

Whenever you are able to distract Spike from a negative behavior (either by making a sudden noise or tossing something toward him), you have a chance to establish some control. Once Spike is distracted, you can talk to him, clap your hand, and so on. Then you are able to move him out of that area and closer to you. In addition to establishing some control over Spike and the situation, it is a nonphysical way to stop Spike from continuing something you did not want him to do and to seem like a benevolent leader to him. This is a way to shape Spike rather than always reacting to what he just did. Reacting and punishing Spike will eventually teach him not to do something, but it will take longer than shaping the correct behavior from the beginning.

Whenever Spike does something that you feel he needs to be corrected or punished for, try to find a related action that you can praise Spike for doing. If he nips, scold him. When he licks you, praise him. If he runs wild through the house, get him to settle down beside you and then praise him. If he likes to constantly pick up items, take advantage of the situation to have Spike pick up the house for you. For every action you do not want Spike to continue, you should try to find something you do want him to continue to do. This way Spike will still try to please you and not constantly ignore you because all you ever seem to do is yell at him.

If you feel the need to correct Spike, usually the simplest and mildest form is best. You don't ground a ten-year-old child for two weeks for not picking up his/her toys (at least not as a first-time punishment). The penalty should fit the crime. It is much better to get tougher with Spike if all other methods fail to produce the desired results than it is to be too harsh in the beginning and have nowhere to go. If you are too harsh, you may make him afraid of you. Or if you lighten up the penalties after a harsh one, he may think you are afraid of him and become even more unruly.

If you have corrected him more than three times for the same offense and he is not getting better, he is not getting the message! Find another method of discipline!

Chapter 11

Safe Toys

Toys for Spike should not resemble articles of clothing or shoes. If you give your puppy an old shoe, how is he to tell the difference between the old one and the pair you just bought for $75? Your puppy should only have two to three toys out on the floor at any one time. He should have a favorite one that he gets when you put him in his crate. This toy is only given to him when you leave, then taken away and hidden when you come home. This way, he won't mind you leaving him quite as much. Too many toys and a dog doesn't seem to play or chew on any of them; he can't seem to make up his mind about which one to choose. It can also cause him to chew on one for a few minutes and then go on to another one for a few minutes and on and on and on. Thus, he will then get bored and want to be entertained. If you have quite a few toys for Spike, put some away and save them for when he is bored with his current toys. Having a dozen or more toys and rotating them helps make the toys last longer and keeps Spike interested in playing with them. None of them should be small enough so that he could swallow them. Toys have more value when the owner plays with the toy and Spike. He who controls the toy is the one in charge!

Hard Chew Toys

Safe toys include the Nylabone. It is made up of nylon particles and formed into hard rings, bones, and knots, in various sizes and shapes. They come in a few different flavors and will usually last for months and months. (They are usually safe unsupervised EXCEPT when they get chewed down to a smaller size.)

The "Roarhide" Nylabone is a great "bone" for pups to teeth on because the pup can actually chew pieces off. (While edible, it is not safe unsupervised when chewed down to a size that Spike can swallow whole.)

Dental Plaque Attackers are of slightly softer material that dogs can chew a little more easily. These also come in various sizes and shapes. As they can be worn down faster (though still taking months to do so with most dogs), start with a larger size than you think necessary for your dog. (Again, they are safe unsupervised until chewed down to a size that Spike can swallow whole.)

The Hercules Bone is similar to the Nylabone, but it has nubs on it, like the plaque attacker. It takes longer for the dog to chew pieces off. As with any of these bones, if a piece breaks off, most dogs do not swallow it. If Spike does, the gastric juices in the dog's stomach will blunt its edges; it will then pass through the dog without problems, unless he manages to swallow too large a piece. Most dogs cannot do this to the Nylabone family of dog chews. But if your dog can, the Galileo bones by Nylabone are super strong and are safe unsupervised, until chewed down to a size that Spike can swallow whole.

If your pup will not chew on a Nylabone, give it to a friend whose dog does chew on them. Once it has been broken in, get it back and give it to your dog. Sometimes they need a little help understanding what they are to do with it. Scented ones may need to have short grooves made in them with a heavy knife. Place them on a cookie sheet in the oven at 350 degrees for a few minutes. This will help bring out the scent of the bone and the pup/dog will take more of an interest in it.

Kongs are really heavy duty rubber in a cone shape. It is very unusual for a dog to be able to chew one apart. Kongs bounce in unpredictable moves, so dogs like to chase them. As they are hollow in the center, they make good pacifiers when leaving puppies or dogs alone. Put peanut butter or squeeze cheese in the opening and leave it with the dog in an area that can be cleaned up easily (putting this filled toy on a rug may result in stains on the rug). This will keep him occupied for a while. It also works great as a distraction when trying to teach the pup about days off of work and being able to sleep later. Kongs come in different sizes and two colors: red and black. The black ones are slightly tougher than the red ones. The King Kong is 6 inches tall and larger breeds like it more than the Labrador retriever-size breeds. (A Kong is safe when unsupervised if it is large enough or not being ripped apart.)

Water Kong has a rope handle imbedded in it so that you can toss it into the water as a retrieving toy. It also has a more spongy interior; so don't let Spike sit down and try to get at the insides.

Booda Bones are ropes of varying lengths and thickness with a knot at each end. Puppies and dogs like to chew on these and shred them. They must be taken away before the dog is able to swallow the fibers. These can get balled up in the stomach and not passed. Only surgery will remove them. Long ones are good for playing tug-of-war. (It needs to be taken away when it starts to fray or it has been chewed down to a smaller size.)

Rawhide bones give the puppy/dog something to chew on and really works his jaws. The only rawhide bones recommended are the compressed ones. They last longer, and the dogs usually cannot get large pieces off of the bone. These large pieces can get stuck in the dog's throat, causing choking problems or even death. Flavored or colored rawhide has contributed to bad behavior in some puppies/dogs. (It seems to be the old Dr. Jekyll/Mr. Hyde syndrome—fine one minute and aggressive the next. Colored milk bones can do it too. Some dogs react to preservatives and/or food coloring by becoming aggressive.) Rawhide should only be given to Spike when you are around to make sure he does NOT bite a large piece off. The thin sticks of rawhide are not suitable except for small dogs, and even then they should be watched while chewing the rawhide in case it needs to be taken away before it causes any problems. The rawhide chips that are sold in bulk in stores also call for supervision when Spike is chewing on them. They can easily slip down the dog's throat and cause problems. Rawhide toys with knots at each end are the easiest for Spike to soften and chew off the entire end; thus, there is a much greater risk of the knot getting stuck in his throat and choking the dog to death or getting stuck inside him and needing surgery to remove it. (Rawhide toys with knots are definitely not safe when unsupervised. Even the compressed ones should be checked often to see how much Spike has been able to chew off.) Rawhide offers a good way to teach a puppy to chew on items that you give him because he is able to soften up the rawhide without a lot of effort. Caution: Bleached rawhide may cause Spike to vomit and or have diarrhea.

A real bone can cause a dog to be more protective about his property when you try to take it away from him. Cooking a real bone makes it soft and more prone to break apart and splinter. These pieces may wedge in the dog's mouth as well as cause minor problems such as irritating the bowel track and causing bleeding or constipation. Any sliver that he gets off and swallows will stay SHARP all the way through the dog, with the potential of piercing of an organ and requiring emergency surgery. Only large thigh bones or marrow bones are appropriate. The ring of a ham bone in a flat slice of ham has been caught over the bottom jaw of smaller dogs. Steak, fish, chicken, and lamb bones are all too soft when cooked; they break and splinter too easily to be safe. Only give raw bones to Spike; and be there to supervise in case Spike has any problems. The bones sold in dog supply catalogs are not nearly as good for your dog as a regular marrow bone from the grocery store or butcher shop.

If you do give a real bone to your dog, teach Spike to chew on it while you are holding it. After thirty or so seconds, take it away from him. If he is good about having it taken away, let him chew on it some more. After a few times like this, put him on a leash, with your foot on the end of it. Then let him have the bone for only a minute or so. When you take the bone away from him, offer him something in return. With your foot on the leash, he cannot take off with it to go under a table or in a room with a carpet (which the bone could stain). He is also less likely to defend the bone with you right beside him. Or you can put him in his crate, give him the bone, and then, when you let him out of the crate, take the bone from him. Make sure he leaves the crate first before you reach in and get the bone. Otherwise he will have a reason to defend both his crate and his bone.

Beefy Baseballs are dimpled like a golf ball but hard like a baseball. They come in two different sizes and colors and are virtually indestructible and float. DO NOT attempt to throw them for Spike to catch; they are heavy enough to hurt his mouth or even snap off a tooth.

Soft Chew Toys

Squeaky toys should be allowed only when you are around to supervise how the puppy plays with the toy. Once a pup learns to like playing with a squeaky toy, he might drive you crazy jumping on it to hear it squeak. Others like to carry them around and gently mouth them to hear them squeak. Some vinyl squeaky toys have a squeaker that can be easily torn out and swallowed. Since some of the squeakers are still made of metal, these toys are not safe! Also, if the puppy/dog chews a large piece loose and swallows it, it may get stuck trying to pass through the dog. Supervising and checking the toys periodically should prevent any problems.

Fleece-type squeaky toys are a big hit with some puppies and dogs. Others just want to rip them apart, in which case you must be very watchful that they don't swallow either the outside fabric or the stuffing. They are great for playing fetch in the house. They can be washed and dried in your laundry machines, and they come in many sizes and shapes. If you have a dog who always wants to carry around a stuffed animal, a fleeced toy will suit his needs. A great source for stuffed toys are thrift stores—very inexpensive with a great selection. Make sure to wash them before giving them to Spike. (This may not be safe when unsupervised.)

Rag dolls and sock babies are toys made out of old socks. Dogs like to carry them around and play tug with them. The biggest drawback to these toys is that most dogs don't distinguish between old socks and your new pair to play tug-of-war with. (They are safe when unsupervised ONLY if the dog does not rip it apart.)

Make sure soft toys do not have any hard parts that can be chewed off. These hard parts include button eyes, noses, and so on.

It is very easy to chew off pieces of the Gumabone, and it does not last very long at all—about an hour for a five-month-old Lab pup. It is a good first bone for pups and small dogs, as they feel they are getting somewhere when they chew on it. (Gumabones are not safe unsupervised when chewed down to a size that Spike can swallow or when Spike is able to chew off pieces small enough to swallow and big enough to get stuck.)

Booda velvets are firm chewable "bones." They are cornstarch based and come in different colors and flavors. Dogs are able to chew them up in minutes. They might be good for young puppies and small breed dogs (though some dogs get diarrhea from them). Care should be taken when giving these to a dog. Watch out for large chewed-off pieces.

Hard rubber toys can have large pieces chewed out of them by even very little puppies and dogs. They are okay in the beginning to teach the pup to chew on something, but keep an eye on how much is being chewed off. Once a pup really starts to chew on this type of toy, you need to be very watchful, as it can be chewed very small in a very short time—even in twenty minutes or so.

With any toy, observing the condition of the toy and taking it away from the puppy/dog BEFORE it gets to be a hazard is the right thing to do. With fleece-type toys, dogs can chew and tear them apart and swallow the stuffing while you are reading a book or watching TV. Some rawhide chewies can be easily and quickly softened and swallowed. Again, the danger is that a large piece will be swallowed and get stuck. As mentioned earlier, bleached rawhide can make dogs vomit or have diarrhea. And pigs ears and hooves and other animal parts sold as chewies are sometimes treated with formaldehyde, which can be toxic!

Fetch Toys

Frisbees come in a variety of materials and are great for exercising Spike while you stand or sit still. Regular frisbees and the ones from Nylabone are harder for a dog to pick up off the ground. They can also hurt his teeth when he tries to grab them out of the air. (This is the type though used in frisbee competitions.) The flexible cloth frisbees are easier on Spike's mouth, and he can pick them up off the ground with ease.

Tennis balls/racquet balls are used often to exercise the dog either by having him retrieve them or by letting him exercise his jaws when chewing on them. If you hit the ball with a tennis racquet, it will go further, thereby tiring Spike out even faster. Be very certain that the ball is large enough that it can't be swallowed. If the dog is able to peel the wrapping off the tennis ball, then he should not be allowed to have one if he is alone. Racquet balls, when made slimy, can go down Spike's throat very easily. Wash brand-new tennis balls in the washing machine before giving them to the dog. The chemical smell on a new ball may be poisonous to the dog! (They are not safe when unsupervised.)

Educational Toys

Buster's Cube and Buster's Ball are two toys that will keep Spike entertained and make him work for his meal. The cube holds approximately 1 to 1-^{1}/$_2$ cups of dry dog food. The ball holds about 4 cups of dry dog food. The amount of food that comes out of either toy can be adjusted. You may have to help Spike in the beginning to learn that by knocking the cube over or rolling the ball, food comes out. As Spike gets better at turning the cube or ball to get his food, make the opening more narrow so that he has to work longer to get the reward. These toys are GREAT for dogs that act up when their owners leave them. There are generic types that are less expensive and come in a few different sizes so that all sizes of dogs are able to work these balls. Keeping Spike mentally stimulated is a way to tire him out. This type of toy is also excellent for rainy days when Spike is driving you nuts. Just put his meal in the container and have him work to get it out.

These are only a few of the toys available for puppies and dogs. Before buying a really expensive toy, ask the vet or your friends if they have had any bad experiences with that particular toy. Also, don't buy a twelve-week-old Lab puppy a chew toy more suitable for a miniature poodle. Within a few more weeks, the Lab pup will be able to swallow a toy of that size. The opposite is true too; don't buy a twelve-week-old Lab pup a toy that a full grown Great Dane would chew on. It will be too big for him and he will lose interest.

All toys and play should be supervised, especially if children are playing with the dog. It is too easy for things to get out of hand and for someone or the dog to get hurt.

Chapter 12

Safe House

Bringing Spike into your home means taking some time to puppy proof your house as much as possible to prevent possible injury to Spike. The more potential problems you can anticipate, the fewer you are likely to have.

Establish off-limit areas until you know how trustworthy Spike is. Either use gates to keep him in the area you want or put a "snake" (i.e., a draft stopper—typically used under closed doors) across the door threshold and teach him not to cross it. A crate will work for short periods of time. Eventually, he will need to learn what his limits are—something he cannot do while confined in a crate. Only when he has learned these limits and will behave should he be allowed loose in the house when no one is home to supervise him.

Baby gates work as well with most dogs, just as they do with babies. They may be less expensive to purchase in a children's store than in some dog supply catalogs. Putting up a baby gate in doorways or to the upstairs will help contain your puppy/dog to the area you want him in. Try keeping Spike in one room barricaded with a baby gate with you in another room. If he climbs or jumps over it, at least you were home to make sure he does not get into trouble. Start off with more limitations than you may eventually want. It is easier to grant new liberties, such as being allowed in more rooms, than it is to keep taking away most of his privileges. He will only try harder to get over the gate.

Tethering him with a chain leash to a mopboard (baseboard) in an area out of the flow of traffic also will work. The leash needs to be attached to a rugged hook in the baseboard so that it cannot be pulled out. Spike cannot chew apart a chain leash. It will give him a chance to get up and stretch his legs and move around more than being in a crate, and it may not seem as confining to him. Tethering may not work in your home if you do not have a space big enough to allow Spike to stretch without being able to reach something to chew on.

While tethering works for some animals and in some instances, it is not recommended as the first thing to try to contain Spike. With sensitive, jumpy, or busy dogs, it can create more behavioral problems than it helps.

Put a "snake" (draft stopper) across the doorway and teach Spike not to cross it. Even though it is used to stop drafts from coming in under closed doors, a lot of people use them to show dogs a barrier that should not be crossed over. It is easier to walk over a snake than it is to keep opening and closing a gate, stepping over a gate, or having to remove it completely each time you want to go through that doorway.

Scat mats are battery operated vinyl mats that give a feeling like a static shock when an animal (or a person in bare feet) steps on it. This mat can be placed in front of doorways, trash cans, plants, counters, and so on, to help keep the animals away from that particular area.

Most dogs are garbage hounds. They will eat anything and everything! Even things you don't think of as edible like panties, socks, candles, soap (some kinds can kill a dog), and cigarette butts. It is better to dog proof your home until he shows you that he is past that behavior. Keep the toilet lid down, especially if you use an automatic toilet bowl cleaner. Even the ones that are "safe if swallowed by animals" have been known to make an adult dog very sick. Think of what they might do to a pup.

Pick up the garbage/trash containers when leaving a dog alone in the house (this is good management). Until you know you can trust him, why take the risk of coming home to a dog that needs surgery to remove a bone, caught in his throat, that he got out of the garbage. Tinfoil and plastic wrap do enormous harm to the intestinal tract. Surgery is usually needed in these cases also.

Watch what the dog can pull off counters or tables. That box of candy can be fatal to your dog! Most dogs cannot tolerate theobromine, an ingredient found in chocolate—it is poisonous to them. Caffeine, another ingredient in chocolate, is not healthy either.

The majority of houseplants are poisonous to dogs. When in doubt, keep the plant out of the dog's reach. If the dog has chewed on a plant, call your vet or the poison control center to see how to deal with the problem.

Puppies eating household soap may also be poisoned. Several soaps that have bactericidal ingredients in them are especially harmful if ingested.

You may want to keep hydrogen peroxide or ipecac syrup on hand in case you need to make the dog vomit. Just a tablespoon of hydrogen peroxide is enough to make a forty-pound dog vomit, usually. If your vet tells you to make the dog vomit, however, give Spike the solution tablespoon by tablespoon until you get the desired results. Make sure to allow him to swallow in between doses; otherwise he may inhale the solution and end up with pneumonia.

Low windows, either basement or low-house windows, are just the right height for the average-sized dog to try to get in or out. Screens do NOT stop a determined dog. Even if the dog seems trustworthy, do not leave him home alone with fully opened windows. Another dog going by, a squirrel or rabbit, a child on a bike, and someone coming to the door are all reasons for a dog to try to get out a window and check out the situation.

Electrical cords should be out of reach, either tucked under the rugs, taped to the baseboards, and so on. It has been known to happen that a year old dog who had never chewed ANYTHING decided to chew the plug off the refrigerator. Thankfully, the dog unplugged it first, or he would have been electrocuted. A puppy or small dog biting an electrical cord, depending on the voltage, will either get a good shock that will burn his mouth or be killed. Electrical cords are NOT to be taken lightly!

Watch where you store your sponges and cleansers. Some dogs just love to open cupboard doors and chew up the steel wool or Brillo pads. Until you fully trust your puppy/dog, you might want to consider putting a baby lock on cupboards containing cleaning supplies.

When Christmas time rolls around, you may want to put the tree into a corner of the room and secure it there, if Spike is still young and bouncy. Put nonbreakable decorations on the bottom few limbs of the tree and DO NOT put tinsel where he can reach it. When a dog swallows tinsel, it usually balls up, making it unable to be passed through the dog. It can also nick up the inside of the dog's stomach, causing bleeding and discomfort. Watch out for tree lights, as they get hot and could scorch his coat. Consider putting baby gates around the tree or putting the tree in a room where Spike is not allowed. That way you can decorate the tree the way you want to and keep both the tree and Spike safe.

During birthdays, watch out for children and balloons. Popping a balloon to scare Spike may seem like fun to the children, but it could cause Spike to permanently dislike both balloons and children and related sounds like fireworks. Spike does not need any cake either—or you may be up all night with a sick dog.

Above all else, if Spike is not trustworthy yet to be left alone, why do so! You can be guaranteed to replace at least one piece of furniture if Spike is left alone in a room when he is not mature mentally enough to handle the responsibility. You can take him with you if it is not too hot or cold out and he won't chew the car. You can crate him. You can take him to doggy day care.

Add the vet's phone number and also the poison control number to your phone book. Better to be ready for any emergency than to not be able to find the numbers when you really need them. Also find out whether your vet does his/her own after-hours emergencies or refers them to an emergency clinic. Add that number to your list and do a dry run to the facility. Do it in both daylight and nighttime so that you know how to get there quickly and not get lost.

Again, the best solution is to be prepared and have the house as free of potential problems as possible. Minimize your use of extension cords or have them go through PVC piping until Spike grows up. Make sure breakables are not within easy reach. Put baby gates up to block him from crawling behind the couch or other pieces of furniture. Add baby locks to those cupboards or storage areas that hold paints, household cleaners, food, and so on. Yes, Spike could pig out on food and have, for example, diarrhea, vomiting, seizures, or a stomach torsion. Better to have everything safe from Spike and Spike safe from everything. These will only be temporary measures until Spike grows up and becomes trustworthy. Better a little inconvenience in the beginning than to have Spike injured or possibly killed.

You may need to periodically review, evaluate, and change how you are keeping Spike and the house safe from each other. Bringing in a new toy for a child may need a time frame of when the child can play with it (when Spike is outside or napping in his crate) or what room it is okay to use it in (perhaps one Spike is not allowed into). Spike will know the difference between an old toy and a new one, new shoes and old ones; they smell different. What smells different must be investigated—usually by him putting it in his mouth.

Having a safe house is one of the most important aspects of good management.

Chapter 13

Safe Games

Playing with your puppy or dog is an important part of his education. Playing properly—not teasing—will teach Spike what is allowed and what is not. If you make a sudden movement, Spike might go into a play bow. This is his signal that he wants to play. Do you? If you don't, he may leap up, nip at you, and leap back as further enticement. This is what he would do with another pup or dog who at first acted as if he wanted to play and then turned his back and started to walk away. Another reason why Spike nips at children is that he is trying to encourage them to play with him. He does not understand that nipping is a no-no.

Chasing someone around the house is not a safe game. The dog will try to catch the person by either tripping or nipping at him/her. A puppy/dog may trip a small child near a table with a sharp corner, causing injury to the child. A large child may trip over a puppy, causing injury or a perceived threat to the puppy (a perceived threat could result in Spike biting the child). Also, chasing Spike is a great way to teach him NOT to come when called. After all, you are always going to him, why should he learn to come to you?!

Playing catch in the house is not a good idea. The dog's feet may slide on the floor surface, causing him to bang into and possibly tip over furniture. This can scare or injure the dog. A dog can also end up with wrenched joints and a sore back from trying to catch the toy and avoid a crash. Never mind the fact that someone's aim may be off!

Non-Busy Games

"Hold the biscuit on your nose" is a typical trick to teach your dog. Many dogs are chow hounds, so this one could take some time! The goal is to have him balance a small dog biscuit on his nose and then wait for a command and/or signal from you to toss it and catch it. He can't have it unless he catches it. If he misses the object, you need to be ready and able to snag the biscuit before he does. Only when he catches it is he able to eat it. He will learn very quickly that he must be quick and accurate with his mouth.

Roll over, shake hands, beg (or sit pretty), and speak are tricks that can be taught easily with just a little time each day.

Roll over. Have Spike lie down so that both his front legs are out straight with his head up and his hind end has one hip rolled under. Take a very tasty treat, let him nibble on it, and *slowly* move the hand with the treat. You want to move Spike's head to the opposite shoulder of the side of the rear that is down. If his left hind leg is under him, you want to have his head go to his right shoulder. By now he will start to lean backward. Keep slowly moving the treat, letting him have a nibble once in a while, until he starts to roll. Once he goes over, maybe with a little help from you, give him lots of praise and the treat. Eventually, once he understands the trick, name the action and use a hand signal at the same time. Spike will be able to understand both with a little more work.

Shake hands. With Spike sitting in front of you, gently cup the elbow of one of his front legs and slide your hand down his leg until you reach the paw. As you are sliding your hand down his leg you are also lifting it slightly off the ground. Once you are at his paw, tell him "Good Shake" or "Paw" or whatever you want to call this action. Put his foot back down on the floor; don't just drop it. Repeat this a few times a training session, but do it as often throughout the day as possible.

If Spike likes to use his feet to paw things or bat things around, here is an even simpler way of teaching this command. Sit on the floor with Spike, who should be sitting also. Feed him about five to seven treats, one at a time, telling him what a good boy he is. Than stop and ignore Spike. Usually he will paw at you to have you resume feeding him. When that happens, reward him again and name the action. With repetitions, he will soon be shaking hands.

Beg or sit pretty. Back Spike up to a corner and have him sit with his back to the two walls. Dangle a really special treat in front of him and *slowly* raise it up in front of his face. Let him nibble on it a bit. With his back supported by the two walls, he should sit up for a few seconds. Give him the treat and praise him. Once he understands how to balance his body, try to have him do this a little distance from the corner or against a piece of furniture. Again, with repetition, he should do fine with this one. Some dogs with long backs are not able to hold this position for very long as it puts quite a bit of pressure on their spine or may cause spasms in their back muscles. This is not a trick for puppies of large breeds; they are usually too clumsy to be to be able to hold the position for any length of time.

Speak. Teach Spike to "Speak" on command, if you haven't already done so. Some dogs don't get into barking to protect the house until they are almost a year of age. If Spike hasn't barked much yet, wait awhile before trying to teach this one. If Spike is not much of a barker, your chances of being able to say the command word on a regular basis is just not there. If Spike has begun to bark almost daily, now is the time to teach this command word. Just decide what the command word will be and wait until Spike barks. Then say the command word as soon as he *stops* barking. Praise him for doing this. If he starts up again, say the command word again and more praise. If he gets out of control, just turn your back on him and ignore him.

Play dead, roll over, shake hands, beg, sneeze, pick up, scratch your back, and stretch or bow can all be taught when the dog makes these moves naturally. With enough repetitions and positive reinforcement, the dog will perform the actions on your command.

Busy Games

Teaching a pup to retrieve in the house on a floor that is carpeted is okay, either by rolling the ball or a low toss. If the pup does not bring the ball/toy back to you but instead goes off to another area of the room, go sit in that area. If Spike consistently goes back to that area, he will start to learn to bring you the toy, rather than you going after him to get the toy back. Once he is fairly reliable about bringing the toy back to you in that area, slide a foot or so to one side and gradually work your way around the room so that no matter where you are when you roll the ball/toy, Spike will retrieve it and bring it back to you.

Teach him the name of a toy and then teach him the "Find?" game. Take one toy and place it a little ways away from you. Tell him to "Find [whatever the toy's name is]." As he gets better, move the toy further and further away until he is going into other rooms or from upstairs to bring you the toy. Once he has mastered that one, name another toy and get him to bring that one to you. Pretty soon you can amaze your friends with your dog's intelligence.

Hide-and-Seek is as much fun for puppies (and dogs) as it is for kids! At first, hide with most of your body NOT hidden by the piece of furniture you are behind. Say the dog's name and even "Come" (just once!) if you want or say something like "Where am I?" Once you hear him trying to find you, make squeaky noises, snap your fingers, clap your hands, drum on the floor—in short, anything to get him to come find you! When he does, he deserves a big reward, lots of patting, snuggle time, massage time, and so on. As he gets better at finding you, hide in more out of the way places, such as a closet. At first, leave the door mostly open; as he gets better at checking out these areas, gradually almost shut the door so that he really has to work to check and see if you are there. A child can hide, for example, in the bathtub, under the sink, or in a laundry basket. If you have two floors to your home, play hide-and-seek on both floors and tire Spike out faster.

Teach him the names of everyone in the family. This can be useful if someone becomes sick or is recovering from an illness or injury. The dog can be taught to deliver messages, keys, mittens, and other light objects. Start by having two people in the same room. Name the other person and tell the dog to "Go see so and so." If the dog won't leave you, turn your back on him. The other person is now the friendly one, and it won't take him long to go to that person. He will need a reward of some sort to want to continue this. Send him back and forth just a few times and then take a break. Do this each day, if possible. Once he has learned two people, teach him a third—if there is another person at home. Teach one person at a time, after the first two, to avoid confusing him.

Games such as say your prayers, read the book, and jump over the other dog or kneeling person can be taught by helping the dog do what it is you want him to do, naming it, praising him for doing it, and then repeating the sequence.

Playing tug-of-war and letting a bold, confident, dominant dog "win" the object more often than you do sets you up for failure as the leader. On the other hand, it is a great confidence booster to have an insecure dog win more than you do. Playing serious tug-of-war before the dog's adult teeth come in could cause Spike to dislike the game. When the game has ended, who has the object? If it is the confident pup more times than not, he will gain even more confidence and power. Most dogs do not understand the words *game over* or *finished* when applied to tug-of-war games. All the dog knows and understands is who ever ends up with the object two parties were trying to retain ownership of is the winner.

Remember, a pup learns by playing games. Is the dog training you or are you training the dog? With any training, whether for obedience, tricks, fieldwork, agility, and so on, the dog learns by repetition and reward. If you do too many repetitions in a row, the dog becomes bored, and his performance will lessen with each repetition. For the best results, keep training sessions short and fun.

If at any time you hear a growl coming from Spike, do not immediately scold or punish him. A growl is your way of knowing something is happening that the dog is not comfortable with. Maybe he has had enough playtime, maybe someone is playing too roughly with him, maybe someone or something is where they/it should not be—whatever the reason, you need to investigate it! To scold the dog for growling will tell Spike that he is always to blame. With some dogs, this means that they will bite someone to tell them that they have had enough rather than warn them with a growl.

There are quite a few more safe games to play with Spike. The extent of his vocabulary and games is only limited by your imagination and time. What if you became temporarily disabled? Teaching Spike to turn on and off the lights (shaking hands/high five), open the fridge, or put the clothes in the washing machine and take them out of the dryer (bring that here, fetch, etc.) can be very helpful. Even though it is help for you, if you treat it right, it is a game to Spike. You never know when you might need Spike's help. By naming as many items as you can that Spike picks up, he will know the difference between your work shoes and sneakers, your jogging pants and work or dress pants, and books, magazines, and newspapers. It's all in how you name it and use it.

With any of these games, once Spike knows the command words, you can teach him a different hand signal for each game or trick.

Just make sure the rest of the family knows exactly how to do the hand signal so as not to confuse Spike.

And it is possible to teach an old dog new tricks; it just may take more time and patience on the trainer's part. This is a way for an older dog to feel part of the family again, for younger children to be able to "train" a dog, and for an older dog to feel that he is just not sleeping out his days and being ignored.

Chapter 14

Positive Identification

Consider having your puppy tattooed and/or microchipped as a way to positively identify him if he is ever lost or stolen. Also, it is against the law for a research laboratory to use an animal that is tattooed or microchipped.

Veterinarians or obedience clubs can usually help you find someone to do tattooing if they themselves do not offer it as part of their services. Tattooing is relatively painless. The instrument is similar to the one used on humans. The dog objects most to being made to hold still while being tattooed (usually on the inside of his upper thigh). There are worldwide organizations that will keep your tattoo number on file in case you lose your dog while traveling or he is stolen. Whoever tattoos your dog can usually supply the forms necessary to register the number.

Veterinarians and some shelters are the only ones who can microchip your dog. The American Kennel Club (AKC) and a major veterinary pharmaceutical company have produced a microchip—called Home Again—that bonds better to the animal's tissue, once inserted between the shoulders, so that it does not move around (this chip is reported to migrate less than the other chips and to have less blanks—shells holding the "chip"). The AKC also put together an 800 phone number and twenty-four-hour hot line. They will register *any* animal that has been microchipped with the Home Again system. It is a little more expensive than the other two systems available, but the AKC has done much more advertising to make the public aware of microchipping dogs and the safety reasons for doing so. They also have a bigger and better staffed registry. All of the microchip companies offer free scanners to animal shelters and humane societies.

Identification tags help dogs get back to their owners if an honest person finds the dog. Otherwise, it is very easy to remove the dog's collar or tags and claim the dog. Be careful about putting your address on the tag. Whoever finds him will know where you live and that you are without your dog. In some areas, this is an invitation to be robbed! Putting the dog's name on the collar can be a reassurance to the dog because he can be called by his name. In place of an address, list two phone numbers so that you are sure of being reached if someone finds your dog. List "Reward" also; this encourages people to give up the dog rather than keep it for themselves or sell it. "Call Collect" or "Needs Meds" also helps encourage the finder to call the owner of the dog.

The best collar to attach tags to is one that the dog will wear whenever he is out of the house, preferably one that buckles or snaps together and is snug enough not to come off over his head easily. If Spike wears a flat buckle collar, tags are available that attach to the collar itself. This type of identification tag does not dangle, so it will not get caught on something, nor will it come loose as easily.

When traveling with Spike, make sure that you have information either in your car, wallet, or purse on what to do with the dog if you are in an accident. Next of kin with phone numbers and addresses should be included for you as well! This can also alert people that Spike is home alone. Be sure to keep all of Spike's vaccinations current, and if he needs medication (e.g., for seizure or heart problems), write it somewhere easily seen in the house, for example, on a calendar or a note on the fridge. Include written certification that Spike has had his rabies vaccination rather than just having him wear his rabies tag on his collar. If he bites someone, you'll have proof that he need not go into quarantine. Some states require proof of a rabies vaccination if you are stopped while traveling through that state!

And finally, do you have a will? What happens to Spike if you go before he does? Don't assume that family members or relatives will do what you want if you have NOT been explicit beforehand.

Chapter 15

Basic Equipment

Do not get caught up in the latest fad when purchasing certain dishes, collars, leashes, and toys. Buy sturdy, durable ones and be sure to check them on a regular basis to make sure they are not worn out or unsafe.

Collars and Leashes

Collars

Collars come in many styles and colors. A buckle- or a martingale-type collar are the **ONLY** types of collars to use if you are going to tie your dog outside. A buckle collar fitted properly should be loose enough to get a couple of fingers between the dog's neck and the collar, yet snug enough that it does not slide over the dog's head when you pull on it. With a puppy, be prepared to buy several collars by the time the pup is full grown. Do not buy a collar that you think will be the final one when Spike is only four months old. It could cause problems—the pup might be able to slip out of the collar, or he might chew on the loose end of it. Always check the collar on Spike every few days. It does not take long for a collar to become too tight and start choking him.

Collars that snap together that look like a buckle collar are fine as long as the dog is NOT a heavy puller on the leash. These types of collars occasionally pop apart when under too much tension; then you have a loose dog.

Training collars, either chain choke, nylon choke or prong, should **never** be used to tie out your dog. If he manages to get a choke collar tightened and cannot get it released, he will choke to death. A properly fitted choke collar should be no more then two inches more than his neck size right up behind his ears. The higher up the collar stays, the more the dog feels it and the less force you will need to exert to correct him. If the collar hangs low on his neck, his strong neck muscles will make most corrections ineffective. If the collar is too loose, he or another dog friend can get a leg through it, and you have an accident waiting to happen. Since some breeds have larger heads then necks, there is a nylon choke collar with a snap. The snap clips to a sliding ring on the collar, and the leash attaches to the ring at the end of the collar. Fitted properly, this collar should be as high up on the dog's neck as it can be. It should be almost difficult to snap the clip to the ring, due to the snug fit. A prong collar will not choke a dog, but if he is tied out with one on, he can, over a period of time, cause the prongs to pierce his skin and become imbedded in his flesh, resulting in a nasty and painful infection. All of these collars work effectively in the right hands. *They should be put on the dog to train him and taken off when finished.*

A choke collar should NEVER be put on a dog under six months of age. If the pup is pulling that hard and is being choked while pulling, he can permanently damage his trachea. He will cough and sputter the rest of his life whenever any pressure is put on his throat. Puppies of the smaller breeds are prone to this problem already and don't need a choke collar to escalate the problem.

If a pup is pulling that hard, try a prong collar or head halter. Be aware that at certain ages, the prong collar may increase a dog's defensive attitude toward people or other animals. *OR* dangle something from your hand to entice him to walk beside you.

A "combination" collar is a martingale collar. It has a ring at each end of the fabric. Another shorter piece of fabric goes through the two rings and is sewn together. A ring is sewn into the shorter piece to attach a leash. When fitted properly, this collar is impossible for a dog to back out of or slip off over his head when tightened.

Any type of collar can choke a dog to death if he gets himself hung up by it! The rings of the collar or the collar itself can get caught on a piece of broken wire in a wire crate or on a chain-link fence. Tags on the collar can slip between the boards of a deck, turn, and get caught. When the dog tries to get up and can't, he may panic and break his neck. Tags can also pass through a wire crate when the dog is resting; when Spike tries to get up, the tags may not come back through into the crate. A panicky Spike inside a crate is a tough situation. You may want to consider the worst case scenario for your dog and your lifestyle and think about whether you want to leave a collar on your dog when no one is home to check on him.

A "no pull" harness is a choice for some people with dogs that pull a lot. This a collar that sits low on the dog's neck with lines that go from the front of the neck, down the front of the chest, behind the dog's front legs, up to the top of his shoulders, to the back of the collar. The leash attaches to the top of the lines. When the dog pulls, the harness changes his center of gravity, and he thinks he is going to fall over onto his nose. You should be aware that short-haired dogs that pull a lot when going for walks may be rubbed raw in the armpit area from the lines. A new harness called a "Holt" or "Coastal" harness does not rub as much on a dog, yet works on the same principles. Also, if not properly fitted, a harness may restrict Spike's gait and make walking any distance uncomfortable. Even if it is tightened as much as possible, Spike can still back out of it. Dogs with coughing problems due to collapsed tracheas need to wear either a harness or a halter to avoid pressure being applied to their neck, making the coughing worse.

Using a head halter on a dog that is taking you for a walk is like having power steering. The "Promise" or "Gentle Leader" types have only two loops, one to go over the nose and the other to be fitted behind the ears. With either of these models, if the nose loop comes off and the back loop is fitted properly, you will not have a loose dog. The dog cannot walk faster than his head is going, so if you keep his head close to you, you have control over the dog. This works great for dogs that lunge toward people or dogs during walks. All the other collars and harnesses leave the dog facing what he wants, therefore making him more frustrated for not obtaining what he wants. With the head halter, he turns back and faces you. Now you have a chance to communicate your commands to him and get him away from the situation much more quickly and easily.

An electronic collar is a useful tool in the right hands. This is not a collar to put on your dog to teach him commands! It is for the dog who knows the commands and is either sluggish about doing them or has the attitude of "make me." The electric shock collar allows you the freedom to let the dog get up to a half mile or more (depending on the model) away from you before giving him a command. If he does not "Come," "Sit," and so on, you touch a button on the transmitter and the dog gets a shock. How much depends on the model. This is a way for the owner to retain control over the dog who thinks that because he is so far away the owner is helpless. In other instances, it is overkill, and the dog can be too frightened to ever leave the owner by more than a few yards or not to want to return to the owner. In hunting, lure coursing, obedience, or agility, this is not what you want!

Electric shock collars should first be used on the dog in his own backyard, doing regular commands that he knows such as "Sit" or "Leave It." If he does not respond on the first command, you press the button on the transmitter, and he receives a small jolt. You will be able to see whether this equipment works on Spike or if it scares him out of his mind. Work around familiar locations until he is comfortable with the collar *before* trying the collar in other places.

There are shock collars for dogs that do a lot of barking when left alone. This type of collar has to fit very snugly for the contact points to be able to give the dog a shock when he sets it off. When the dog barks, the vibration of the bark sets off the collar, and he gets a shock. The strength of the shock can be tailored to the dog. WARNING: If another dog or person is around when Spike gets his first shocks, he will blame that animal or person. This may cause Spike to become aggressive toward that animal or person.

While electric collars are included here, they are *not* the author's first choice. Most people use the collars to stop problems they are too lazy to deal with properly! With a little time, effort and imagination, use of shock collars may not be necessary. In the right hands they can be a very effective tool to use short term.

Citronella collars are also for dogs that bark when you do not want them to. This type of collar does not have to fit as snug as a shock collar, because it is the sound of the bark and not the vibration that sets it off. There is a small box on the collar that contains citronella oil. The collar should be positioned on Spike so that the box is under his neck. When Spike barks, it releases a squirt of the strong smelling oil. Spike will usually subside and stay quiet. This does not work on all dogs. Some training centers and veterinarians rent the collars for a small fee per week for people to try on their dogs.

Leashes

Leashes should be made of cotton or leather. A chain leash will peel skin off your hands if your dog bolts. A nylon leash will give you a burn if the same thing happens. Wide, double layered nylon is often too bulky to hang onto comfortably—so the dog gets to pull more, and the owner experiences discomfort and cuts on the palms of his/her hands. Do not allow Spike to chew on the leash; it could weaken and then break—just when you need to give a fast tug on the leash to bring him back away from a potentially dangerous situation.

Do not get a leash for a full-grown dog and put it on your puppy's collar. The snap of the leash will be too big and heavy, and it can hit him in the face, making him not like being on the leash. Buy leashes and collars proportioned to your dog's size.

Flexi-leads are fine for quickly running the dog outside to go to the bathroom. While they are retractable, they are a nuisance to use around a lot of people, dogs, bushes, and trees, as the dog seems to enjoy tangling the leash up as much as possible. I've known of several people who have had their palm sliced open from grabbing the line to stop a dog as the brake had broken.

Dishes and Beds

Dishes

Food dishes should be made of stainless steel; it is easier to clean and can be disinfected readily. Crock-type dishes can crack and chip and injure the dog's chin. If the glaze cracks on a crock dish, some of the material it is made out of can be a potential hazard to your dog's health. With poorly made or chipped crock dishes, the risk of Spike getting lead poisoning increases significantly. Plastic bowls are difficult to clean thoroughly, and they harbor bacteria that can cause acne-type problems on the dog's chin. They have also been associated with gum problems in the dog. They are also the easiest for the dog to chew to pieces and pick up. Plastic bowls also tend to turn some dogs's noses from black to a liver-brown or even a pinkish-brown color. A yellow Lab may have a dark brown nose, but when fed out of a plastic bowl, it may turn pinkish.

Beds

What is Spike going to sleep on? Puppies like to chew. If crated and bored, Spike will chew on his bed, even if he has a toy in the crate. Sometimes it is better for Spike to have nothing in his crate until you are sure he will not chew it up.

Some mats for crates are covered in a fabric that is water repellent. Accidents are easier to clean up, but Spike can still chew it. The foam pad used in these mats may be toxic to a very small or a very young puppy.

Dog beds come in various sizes, shapes, fabrics, and colors. Dog beds with poly beads in them as padding are best. They can be washed in the washing machine (if not too large) and dried. Dog beds with cedar chips in them will smell nice in the beginning, and you can add more cedar chips to them as the odor fades. The cedar will help repel fleas from the bed. Having a bed with cedar or pine shavings in it makes it difficult or impossible to wash, so don't use one with a puppy that isn't completely housetrained. If a dog urinates on it, you might never be able to get the smell out, no matter what you pour on it. (In the case of two or more dogs, one might urinate on it to mark it as *his* bed.)

Using a bed sheet over the cover keeps the cover cleaner longer. It is easier to take off the sheet and wash it than it is to take off the cover of the bed. You can also change your color with little effort or expense! If you want to have Spike sleep in a wicker basket or other type of framed dog bed, wait until he is over a year of age. By that time, he will be done with chewing everything in sight. If you are going to allow Spike on the furniture, putting a cover sheet over it will keep the furniture cleaner and more free of odors. Again, it is as simple as buying a new bed sheet to change the color scheme.

Remember the size of the dog you are buying for. Make sure the toys, collars, leashes, bed, bowls, and so on, are in keeping with his size, or Spike won't enjoy them. And dogs do learn what different collars and harnesses mean. Thus, a flat buckle collar may mean a ride in the car, an orange collar may mean field work, a chain choke collar may mean obedience competition time, a nylon choke may mean competition time in the confirmation or show ring, and a harness may mean tracking or hauling you around while you are on snow skis. The dog can understand all the different uses as long as you teach him what each one means and are consistent with the use of them.

Chapter 16

Fences and Exercise

In these days of leash laws in almost every town and/or state, be a good neighbor and keep your dog on his home turf. You can turn good neighbors into bad neighbors very fast by allowing your dog to go to the bathroom on their lawn and not picking it up. No one likes a roaming dog; he tends to cause or get into trouble. In most states, if your dog is loose and causes a car accident, you can be held liable.

When you take your dog for a walk, carry plastic bags along in case he has a bowel movement. You can pick it up with the plastic bag and toss it into the nearest trash barrel, or you can leave it on the side of the road out of the way of traffic and pick it up on your way back from your walk. Your neighbors will appreciate and applaud your efforts. In some places, this is a law.

Try to make sure he does not make a nuisance of himself by barking at everything and anything. He should learn the command "Quiet." Booby traps/shake cans, water pistols, or bark collars can teach him to be quiet. For Spike to understand the command, you need to be saying it when he IS quiet. Telling him to be quiet when he is barking teaches him that the word means to bark!

Fencing

How are you going to leave Spike outside for a while and be sure he is not able to get into trouble? Tying up Spike will keep him from wandering but will not exercise him. Even on trolley line tie outs, dogs will rarely exercise themselves unless something or someone keeps them occupied. Tying is the most economical way to keep Spike from wandering. It does allow, however, other dogs to come into his yard and either attack him or tease him by staying just out of reach. Children in the neighborhood tend to do the same with a tied out dog. They will not fully approach the dog, and he becomes more frustrated each time, to the point where he no longer likes to have kids around him when he is outside and tied up. Do not put the line near the door most often used; if you do, he can become protective about who approaches. Also be sure Spike can reach shade and shelter. Does he have water available or can he knock the container over easily and be thirsty the rest of the day? Hanging a water bucket from a tree or post allows Spike to drink and not tip the bucket over.

A tethered dog **MUST** have an appropriate collar on so that he does not choke himself to death if he should get the line caught around anything. A well fitting flat buckle (not a snap-together collar—it will pull apart under pressure) or a combination collar is the best collar. A flat buckle collar should be snug enough so that you can just get two fingers between the collar and Spike's neck.

A small chain-link portable pen is an okay place to exercise small dogs, but medium to large dogs cannot move around enough. The small enclosure does keep them safe, but they will need more exercise than this!

Fencing in either part of your yard or all of it is a big expense, but then so is the vet bill if Spike gets hit by a car. A fence should be high enough so that Spike does not have the inclination to jump over it. In snow country, it needs to be high enough so that in deep snow with a hard crust, Spike cannot get over it. Either tramp down the borders or shovel the snow away from the fence.

A chain-link fence is very expensive but will last for a very long time. Unless you live where zoning prohibits fences over four feet high, you should plan on making all fences six feet high. An average dog in good shape will go over a four-foot fence! You might be able to keep your small dog inside a four-foot fence, but what about keeping OUT the large dog next door—especially if you have a female dog who is not spayed yet!

Wood fencing looks more attractive around your house, but it will rot, and Spike can chew through it. It will need to be checked on a regular basis for weak areas. Do not leave the boards too far apart; most dogs like to stick their heads through and look around.

An "invisible" fence will cover more area for less money than regular fencing. (It works on almost the same basis as the electric shock collar.) Spike wears a collar with a receiver attached to it. When Spike is within a set distance from the wire in the ground, he receives a warning beep first. If he goes past that point, he then receives a shock. There are drawbacks:

　　　If Spike manages to get out of the fence, he won't want to come back through and be shocked again; therefore, he'll remain loose and in potential danger.

139

- Other dogs can come into his yard and pick a fight.
- Periodically, there will be breaks in the wire, allowing Spike to come and go without getting a shock.
- Spike could become afraid of getting shocked and not want to leave the door.
- The less expensive models have even had the dog receive a shock when he passes by an electrical outlet in the house. What a way to make Spike paranoid!

If you live in a fairly populated area, you may want to think about how many people walk routinely by your house. If Spike gets too close to the fence line when certain people or dogs go by, he could become aggressive toward those animals or people as he gets shocked whenever they are around. Then when Spike is off his property and meets that animal or person, he could go after them—and not in a friendly way.

An electric fence such as one you might use for large animals (e.g., horses or cows) will not work on Spike unless you put numerous strands 4 inches apart and electrify them all.

If Spike is a digger, or becomes one, you need to consider how to stop him from digging out of his yard. You can bury the fence six inches to one foot in the ground; however that leaves you less fence above the ground. As mentioned earlier, an athletic Spike can easily jump over a four-foot fence. You can put one or two feet of chicken wire on the ground and attach it to the existing fence. Crushed rock or logs on top of the wire will discourage Spike from trying to dig out. If Spike is not a digger (yet), adding railroad ties or large logs to the inside boundaries may prevent him from ever trying. Logs can also be placed at the bottom on the outside of the fence.

A shrubbery fence should be put around any shrubs, plants, or trees that you do not want Spike to dig up or chew on. Since most shrubs are poisonous, this is also a safety feature. In addition, you may not want Spike to urinate on any bushes because this will usually kill the bushes.

Putting shrubbery around the outside of Spike's fenced area will help screen dogs and people passing by his property. He may still bark when he hears their sounds—but usually not for as long as he would if he could see them.

Boundary training Spike to never leave the yard works on maybe 1 percent of the dog population. It takes a dedicated owner and the right type of dog to make this training reliable under any and all conditions.

Regardless of the fence or tie out you choose for Spike, leaving him outside while no one is home is not safe. If he is tied out and another dog fights with him, you could come home to an injured dog, or worse. Or he could get caught up around a tree or post and have had only a foot of movement most of the day. In a fenced-in area, Spike could dig his way out, get his collar caught on the fence, or jump/climb over the fence.

Even when you are home, you will need to check on Spike periodically while he is outside. It doesn't take long for an accident to happen and for Spike to need assistance quickly.

There are pros and cons to every type of tie out and fencing. You should take the time and make a list of your needs. The dog must have shade and access to water, maybe even a child's wading pool in the hot weather. Where will you put it? How will it look? What are the zoning requirements? How high and long should it be? What will have access to the dog that could possibly cause him harm? What can he get wrapped around? Where could he possibly dig out?

Surface Material for a Run or Kennel

Whatever type of fencing you use to contain Spike, think for a moment about the type of surface you want under his feet. Cement is the easiest material to keep clean; however, it is a very hard and unforgiving surface that may result in sore joints. It should have a slight slant so that water will drain off. Large breed dogs may develop splayed (wider and flatter) feet from being on cement too long. If Spike likes to jump at the gate to greet you, the constant landing on cement may aggravate any existing joint problems or cause new ones!

Crushed rock drains well, but it makes poop scooping difficult. If you have a dog that digs, using crushed rock around the inside boundary of the fence will discourage him from trying to dig his way out. Too much time on rock may irritate or cut Spike's pads. There are several different sizes of gravel, from over two inches to pea stone. Talk to other dog owners or a person in the gravel business and see what size they recommend. Gravel is a little easier on Spike's feet, but it sinks into the ground faster.

Stone dust makes a nice finished area that is easy to clean; however, it will not drain as well as crushed rock or gravel. In clay areas, rocks, gravel, or stone dust will eventually sink in the ground.

Patio blocks are handy, movable cement pieces that are roughly two by two feet. They can be picked up and moved from location to location as often as you want to change the landscaping of Spike's pen. Patio blocks under and around a wading pool will keep the water clean.

If you have clay soil, adding pine shavings (large animal feed stores sell bales of pine shavings at a very reasonable price) to the soil will thicken it and help it dry more quickly. Then if you want to add, say, crushed rocks, or gravel, the rocks will not sink into the ground as quickly.

If there is grass in Spike's area and mud season is driving you crazy, try putting a light layer of feed hay (cheap green hay that sells for $3.50 to $7 dollars a bale, not timothy hay) on top of the wet areas. If you shake the hay out so that individual strands fall, grass will grow back up through. If you cannot see the ground through the hay, it has been put on too thickly and will kill the grass. Putting a clump of hay into a puddle will not dry up the puddle any more quickly than a light layer. Feed hay will also reseed a large area, so you don't have to fuss with grass seed and mulch.

Exercise

No matter how you keep Spike safe in the yard, he still needs regular exercise. A single dog in a fenced yard will seldom do enough running around to tire himself out (though a dog will exercise himself more in a rectangular yard/area than in a square one). A well-exercised dog is a happy dog and one that does not have the energy to get into trouble. The downside to trying to tire Spike out is that the more he exercises, the more exercise he will require before he tires out. Stamina builds up quite rapidly in a young dog. Be sure he has access to clean water and won't be able to knock it over while he is out in the fresh air.

Walking, Jogging, Biking

Age appropriate exercise is the best way to avoid health problems with Spike. Do not expect the very young or the very old dog to keep up with you for a two-mile walk. While Spike may keep up with you, he may be injuring his growth plates at the end of each bone and end up with one leg that is shorter than the other or more painful. You can work up to that distance *gradually*.

You can walk a longer distance with Spike when he is younger than you can jog with him. Jogging is harder on the dog's joints and should not be done for distances over a half mile until the dog is at least eighteen months of age—or at least twelve months of age with a smaller breed. Young dogs will instinctively try to follow you no matter how far you go; however, they will pay for it in later years by becoming more stiff and sore at an earlier age. All dogs benefit from sensible regular exercise. Check with your veterinarian before starting any jogging or strenuous exercise with Spike.

Adding a piece to your bike that you may attach Spike's leash to is another way to exercise him once he is older. But be careful. Check out the area you will ride for possible hazards (broken glass, cans, metal tabs, small pointed rocks, etc.). Also, check Spike's feet after every biking run. Most dog's pads will turn pink when they run over asphalt. Do short runs (and not every day) until the dog's feet have toughened up. This type of exercise is best done where there is not a lot of confusion, loose dogs, or kids. Spike may try to lunge toward every distraction, leaving you trying to maintain your balance on the bike. Vary your speed while on the bike; this will help Spike to burn up more energy and calories and to build endurance. It also keeps the exercise from being boring for both him and you.

Young dogs and senior dogs do better with shorter walks several times a day. (Yes, this has already been said, BUT it bears repeating because of the number of arthritic middle-aged animals that come into my husband's practice who were once very active and hard running.) Several shorter walks will put less wear on a dog's joints, will be less overwhelming than a longer walk, and will help keep an older dog's muscles more flexible. The more often an older dog can get up and go for a short walk, the less stiff and sore his muscles will become. An older dog that goes for one long walk a day may be too sore or uncomfortable to get up within a few hours after the walk, even to go outside to the bathroom.

Finally any dog that is limping should not go for a walk UNLESS you know that the dog will improve once he gets moving.

Swimming

Swimming is the best way to exercise any age or breed of dog. It allows them to use their muscles without putting weight on their joints. Swimming is especially therapeutic for dogs recovering from muscle, leg, or joint injuries or surgeries. There are some dogs that do not like the water, and throwing them into it is not the way to make them enjoy it. Usually the opposite happens; they become more afraid of a pond or lake. Some breeds like collies do not like swimming, but with patience, they can be taught to enjoy it. Dogs with tails use them as rudders and use their hind legs less, except to maintain the direction they want to swim in. Dogs with no tails or short tails can still swim; they just use their hind legs more. All dogs can be taught to enjoy swimming.

Take Spike and a friend to a body of water that is not too cool. Go out into the water with Spike—but stay in shallow water so that his feet touch the ground. Have your friend call Spike back to shore and give him a really great treat. Then you call him back to you. Keep doing this until Spike is comfortable with being in the water and returning to shore.

Now take Spike out a little further, get him used to floating, turn him so that he faces the shoreline, and have your friend call him in. Again, give Spike a very special treat. Quit while you are ahead and try it again another day. In a very short time, you will have Spike swimming around like a pro. When you want him to retrieve something in the water, first throw it toward the shore while you both are out in the water. Try to get him to return to you. If he does not, next time be in the water but along the shoreline and throw the article to be retrieved along the bank. Spike should then be more interested in bringing it back to you, especially if he receives a treat for doing so. If Spike does not retrieve on dry land, he will not usually retrieve in the water. Work on encouraging him to try it on land first.

If you have a friend who has a dog that is an enthusiastic swimmer, one who leaps off the shoreline, diving for the thrown article, have Spike meet that dog. Watching another dog enjoy a sport, receive attention, and have fun will usually encourage Spike to try to do likewise.

Heavy coated dogs have a harder time getting out of the water repeatedly unless they have been well conditioned. Once their coat absorbs water, they become a lot heavier. Keep an eye on Spike. While he may be an enthusiastic swimmer, you do not want him to tire to the point of starting to sink! If Spike is going to be doing a lot of swimming, you may want to consider trimming/thinning his coat considerably.

Dogs who swim in salt water should be rinsed off as soon as possible to avoid drying out their coats. If not rinsed out, the coat will become stiff with dried salt and make the dog itch.

Dogs who swim in swimming pools should also be rinsed off as soon as you know they are done for the day. You would not want to walk around all day with chlorine on you; neither does Spike. Pool chemicals may not be as "friendly" to Spike as they are to you. It is a safe bet that if you would rinse off your child after being in a hot tub or pool, you should do the same to Spike.

Wherever Spike goes for a swim, do you want to leave his collar and tags on? If he swims in salt water, you will be replacing his collar on a regular basis, as the salt will stiffen up the fabric and make it age faster. Does Spike swim among lily pads and other plant growth? If so, his tags could get caught on a plant. Are you willing to jump in and save him? Even in a pool, Spike could get his collar stuck under the ladder, causing him to panic and maybe drown if no one is around.

Retrieving

Chasing Frisbees or tennis balls can get Spike tired out in a short space of time. However, there are drawbacks to having Spike do a lot of retrieving when he is young. While Spike is chasing a Frisbee or ball, the sudden stops and turns can do damage to his joints and/or ligaments. So keep it to a minimum of retrieves, but do it several times throughout the day, until he is about eighteen months of age. Also watch out for his back. Some breeds are prone to back problems and any catching or retrieving should be kept to a very few catches at a time. Dogs that do a lot of jumping and twisting to catch Frisbees or balls should not do too many in a row before having a rest. You may want to practice your Frisbee throwing before letting Spike go after one. To avoid injury to Spike, keep the Frisbee low and avoid throwing it over rutted ground. There are dogs that are great Frisbee catchers, and they wow any crowd; but they age faster due to the amount of practicing they do, plus their joints are usually quite arthritic before they pass out of middle age. There are Frisbee competitions if you think Spike is doing that well. Check with your local obedience clubs, animal hospitals, and animal shelters to see if there is one being held in your area in the near future. Even if Spike is not ready for it, you can go and pick up some training tips.

If you hit a tennis ball with a tennis racquet rather than throw it, it will go further; thus Spike gets a longer run and may not be doing quite so much twisting and turning to catch the ball. It also cuts down on the number of sudden turns.

Throwing sticks for dogs to retrieve can result in injury to the dog. For example, if Spike grabs a stick that landed upright in the dirt, he could jab himself in the mouth. He may not be very enthusiastic to retrieve it again. Some dogs have gotten sticks wedged into the top of the mouth and needed to see a vet to get it out. Dogs playing tug-of-war with a stick can jab it into the back of the other dog's throat or cause other serious injuries. If the stick gets caught in the earth and part of it stays upright, the dog could get poked in the eye trying to grab it on the run. Or he could jab himself in the mouth. Some dogs have even cracked a molar trying to grab a stick this way.

A canvas bumper or dummy used to teach retrievers to fetch in the water can be used on land also. Some are made with heavy duty rubber/vinyl that is knobby so that dogs won't bite down hard on it. They usually come in white or orange colors. They also come in different sizes and weights.

With any retrieving exercise, end the game BEFORE Spike wants to. This way you will build the desire to retrieve even more strongly. If you keep throwing things for him to fetch and he eventually becomes tired and wanders off, he is in charge of the game. Also, he will end the game sooner each time because he may think you will NEVER stop throwing something for him to fetch.

Games and Digging

Even on rainy days, Spike can be exercised in the house, especially if you have a set of stairs. If you have someone with you, have him/her stand at one end of the stairs while you stand at the other. Call Spike to you, praise him, give him a treat, and send him to the other person. If Spike will not leave you when the other person calls him, turn your back to him and ignore him. Do this a few times and take a break. If you do it too many times in a row, Spike will become bored with the game and want to quit. If you do this too many times in a row with a puppy, you run the risk of the puppy getting tired and falling down the stairs. If you do not have a partner to help you, toss a soft toy up the stairs and encourage Spike to retrieve it.

Hide-and-seek can be played in fields and woods (and in the house on rainy days). By hiding when he is not looking or when he is a little more ahead of you then you like, you teach him to keep an eye on you at all times. Don't allow him to go past you; make a noise so that he has an easy time finding you at first. Then, as he gets better at the game, see how well he uses his nose to locate you. If you hide when he is out of your comfort range (the distance away from you that you are comfortable with), he will learn not to roam too far from you.

Digging in the yard is a form of exercise to Spike. If you don't like where he is digging, you can teach him to dig in one particular spot. If you do not allow a digging dog some place where he can dig, you will probably never stop the habit. So pick a spot in the yard that you will not be as upset over and let him dig. (Do not let Spike watch you plant your garden or work in your flower bed. He will surprise you by digging everything up.)

Take Spike's favorite toy out to the yard along with Spike. With a shovel, dig a very shallow hole and put the toy in the hole. Put a little bit of dirt on top of the toy and tell Spike to "Dig"; encourage him to get the toy. Repeat this until Spike gets a clue to the command. Now, dig a little deeper and repeat the command. Over the course of several days, keep digging the hole deeper and deeper and putting more dirt on top of the toy until only a small part of it is visible. Keep sending Spike out to "Dig" for his toy. His reward is his toy.

Dogs will also dig a hole when they are hot and want to get cool. Alternatives include the air conditioned house, the basement, a wading pool, or wetting a part of the lawn and encouraging him to lie down on it.

Organized Sports

Organized sports can be fun for both you and Spike. They are also a way for you to meet other people who enjoy their dogs.

Flyball is a team sport of at least four dogs. These dogs run one at a time, relay fashion, over four jumps, and catch a tennis ball. The ball is shot out of a box that they trigger when they step on a certain area. Your dog races back over the jumps, and the next dog in line goes. It is a timed event, so the fastest team wins. If your dog is good enough, there are even titles that can be earned.

Scent hurdles is just like flyball in that it too has a team of four dogs that run relay fashion over four jumps. Instead of a box discharging a tennis ball, there is a tray holding four dumbbells. The dog has to pick HIS dumbbell and race back over the jumps, and then the next in line goes. Again, it is a timed event, so the fastest team wins. Both flyball and scent hurdles are great sports to take to schools, nursing homes, and hospitals.

Agility is really an obstacle course with jumps, tunnels, weaving through upright poles, walking a narrow plank, and climbing steep ramps in a race against the clock. There are different organizations with different rules and jump heights. It is great way to gain more control over your dog and still have a GREAT deal of fun and exercise. Check out any competitions near you to see if they are holding any classes that are open to the public.

Lure coursing is a super way to tire out your dog *but* only if he is in good shape! The dog is encouraged to run after a white plastic garbage bag tied to a thin nylon line that moves along a course with the help of spindles and a motor. Someone runs the control to keep the lure in front of the dog enough to keep him chasing it. In competition, there may be two to three dogs running after the lure at the same time. Depending on the size of the dog, the course may be a quarter of a mile long or more. Lure coursing competition is only open to "sight hounds," meaning breeds of dogs such as the greyhound, whippet, Afghan hound, and saluki. These breeds of dogs were originally bred to see an animal off in the distance and be able to run it down and catch it.

Tracking is something all dogs do naturally. When training a dog for tracking, he is asked to follow a particular person to where they dropped a glove or other article. It is an easy, fun, and inexpensive sport. Once the dog understands what you want him to do, you can vary the degree of difficulty by increasing the age (the time between when it was put out and when the dog follows it) of the track, making it longer, or going over different terrain. Most obedience clubs hold tracking clinics. If there is not one in your area, check the attached book list for some reading recommendations to start one yourself. As puppies like to sniff everything, this is a perfect age to start tracking. A dog of any age can learn it though.

While there are competitions and titles for the above events, you do not need to enter one to enjoy the sport. Just enrolling Spike in a class will be enough for him to gain confidence and pride in what he accomplishes.

The American Kennel Club has titles available for many events, such as herding, retriever trials, pointer and beagle trials, terrier work, tracking, lure coursing, obedience, show, junior showmanship, and Canine Good Citizen. Working a dog toward his title is a way to get the whole family involved in planning the shows and how to get there, conditioning the dog, training, and so on.

If you have a purebred that is not recognized by the AKC, see if it is recognized by the United Kennel Club (UKC). Mixed breeds, mutts, All Americans, Heinz 57, designer dogs—whatever you want to call them—can compete for titles through an organization called AMBOR. (Addresses for AKC, UKC, and AMBOR are in the back of the book.)

Nursing home, hospital, and school visits are ways to bring joy to others and show off your dog. Spike needs to be well behaved and usually needs to be a registered therapy dog. Some people in nursing homes who have not spoken for a long time begin to talk again, perhaps about a dog they once had, when a dog comes into their lives. It is a great feeling to bring some pleasure into the lives of the elderly, the sick, or young children. You and your friends can make up a drill team and put on performances for public events and parades.

Remember, a dog who gets enough exercise does not have the energy to be destructive in the house or yard and also has fewer behavior problems. And because you are in control when you interact with Spike, he respects you as a leader.

A WELL-EXERCISED DOG IS A HAPPY DOG!

Chapter 17

Grooming

Begin good grooming habits when your puppy is very young. Let him get used to being touched, fussed over, and inspected for fleas, ticks, and lumps. Pick up his feet and pretend you are going to clip his nails just to get his feet used to being handled. Although his coat may stay short (or not, depending on the breed), brush him on a regular basis, about every other day so that he becomes accustomed to being groomed and does not object. Your breeder, veterinarian, or groomer can tell you the best combs or brushes to use on your dog's coat. While trying to train Spike to allow any grooming, remember to let him off the grooming table periodically for a playtime. Try to time it so that you let Spike off the table just before he has had enough.

Brushing

If Spike will not let you groom him, he is in control, not you. Change how Spike perceives this exercise by making it into a positive experience for him. Put peanut butter or soft cheese on the refrigerator at his face level. Encourage him to lap it off. Once he really starts to work on it, slowly and gently start to brush him. You may only get to do a few brush strokes before Spike gets upset, but that was more than you had been able to do! Wait a few hours and try it again. Eventually, with patience and the right treats, Spike will learn to allow himself to be groomed. The alternative is to take him to a groomer, who will physically force him to stand still and be groomed. The last recourse is to take Spike to a veterinarian for a tranquilizer or even to be anesthetized in order to be groomed. With some dogs, you may have to put them on a grooming table; being up off the ground makes some dogs insecure, so they behave better. You may need to combine the table and the food on the fridge to get positive results. With other dogs, you may need to cross tie them by snapping two leashes to their collars. One gets hooked or tied to a piece of heavy furniture on one side and the other is hooked or tied to another piece of heavy furniture on the opposite side of him. These leashes need to be quite taut so that there is no slack. When cross tied, Spike cannot turn around and snap at you. Take the time to teach your puppy about grooming. It will cost you less in the long run and save Spike and you a lot of stress.

Brushing or combing should be done as often as the length of coat and condition require. When a dog is shedding, brushing or combing several times a day will speed up the process. Shedding occurs in stages. The hair on the dog's back will usually fall out first. About a week after the back has finished shedding, the sides and underneath will start to fall out. If you fail to brush throughout the entire shedding process, Spike may end up with mats that need to be shaved off because they are too close to the skin to cut out. Rather than looking good for the show ring or for company, Spike will look moth eaten and not very handsome. Check for mats between the toes if you have a long-haired breed of dog. If you have a male dog with long hair, be sure to keep the hair short on his underside to prevent urine soaking, which will cause the hair to mat and smell. If you want to show Spike in the conformation ring and need to keep the undercoat long, clean it often and add baby powder to the area. Of course, the powder will help soak up the urine and keep matting to a minimum. The powder will need to be washed off on a regular basis to prevent it from matting to the coat.

Sharp-tined "slicker" brushes can cause discomfort on short-coated breeds of dogs. Be careful how hard you bear down on the brush when using it. The same can be true about a "shedding blade." This looks like a hacksaw blade and on bony areas of the dog can cause scraping of the skin. Wide-toothed combs work great in a variety of coats and do a good job of taking out the dead hair. By having a few combs with different widths between the teeth, you can do almost all of the grooming needed for a medium- to a long-haired breed of dog. Try out a comb or brush on yourself first to know just how much pressure to apply when using it on Spike. If it hurts you, it will probably scratch Spike.

For a short-haired dog, using a "hound" glove (short, tightly packed together bristles or nubs on the palm side of a glove) during his shedding season may be all that it takes. Even for short-haired dogs, a shed n' blade (used lightly around bony areas) will remove a great deal of hair. For some breeds, such as the whippet, Doberman, and Great Dane, just lightly dampening your palms and wiping the dog down with a little pressure will remove a lot of loose hair. You will be able to tell if Spike needs a bath by how much dirt you have on your hands when you are done.

Also good to use on short-haired breeds to hurry along the shedding process is a rubber curry brush. It is almost oval in shape and has two rows of rubber teeth that when used in a circular motion helps release any hairs ready to fall out.

Most of the terrier breeds need to be hand stripped. There are special stripping combs for this purpose. If you cut a terrier coat with electric clippers, the new hair will be softer and will not repel water and dirt as easily. Most pups in the beginning will object to having this done. As the dog gets older and out of the puppy stage, this will be done with less fuss. Also, as the dog grows older, the skin becomes a little tougher and accepting of having the hair pulled out. With patience, playfulness, and treats, Spike will learn to accept hand stripping.

When encountering a mat, be careful cutting it out. If you hold onto the mat and cut as close to the skin as possible, you will probably end up cutting Spike—a justifiable reason to fear and dislike grooming. Some mats that are not very large can be worked apart by adding a little bit of hair conditioner. Work the conditioner into the mat and wait about thirty minutes before trying to work the strands of hair apart. If you do need to cut a mat, hold it with one hand resting on Spike's skin. Place your fingers between the base of the mat and Spike's skin and cut against your fingers, *not* Spike's skin. You can comb out what little bit of hair is left behind. If it is a very large mat, using an electric hair clipper is easier and faster, with less chance of cutting Spike. Removing all mats and tangles BEFORE giving Spike a bath is easier than trying to do so after his bath. Bathing Spike with mats will only make them bigger once he dries off.

It is fashionable for certain breeds to have the hair clipped on the muzzle along with the whiskers. Whiskers should NEVER be clipped on a blind animal because they are part of his sense of touch and help keep him from bumping into furniture or other obstacles.

Dogs with hair between their toes and dragging on the ground may need a trim occasionally. A neat foot brings in less dirt, mud, or snow. Some breeds with hairy feet also get mats between their toes. Check the feet on a regular basis.

Toenail Care

Most dogs need to have their nails clipped about once a month. Some more often; some less often depending on their size and the type of terrain they walk on. A general rule of thumb is that when you can hear the toenails click on the floor as the dog walks, it is time to trim them. Ask your vet or groomer to show you how to trim the nails. Dogs with long toenails run the risk of having them break, tear, or split while they are running. It is better to take off little pieces more frequently than to take off a larger slice and possibly cause bleeding. The first few times Spike has his toenails cut, ask an experienced friend to do it for you. This way, if the nail is cut too short, Spike will not be as upset with you, and you will be able in the future to cut his nails with less of a struggle.

The type of nail clipper you use may be more important to your dog than it is to you. The guillotine-type clipper cuts more cleanly. If you cut the nail from top to bottom or vice versa, it pinches the toenail less; therefore, the dog may tolerate it better. The guillotine-type of nail clipper also has replaceable blades. The pliers-type clipper is usually used so that it cuts the nail side to side, leaving a short ridge behind where the two edges meet. It also pinches the toe more.

Also, there are nail files for dogs; these can be used to file down the ridge left behind from the pliers-type cutters or to smooth out the nail and take away any sharp edges that might catch on things. You use a file on Spike the same way you would use an emery file on yourself.

Dogs with white toenails have quicks (tender flesh at the base of nails) that you can see. You cut almost up to BUT NOT into the pink area.

Dogs with black toenails have quicks that are harder to see. Once you cut the toenail, if you pick up the dog's foot and look straight at the interior of the toenail, you will see a center that is either almost shiny black or more like a soft, speckled black, gray, and white. With the shiny black nail, the closer you get to the dog's quick, the more you will see a change in the texture and color of the nail, usually around the twelve o'clock position on the nail. Cut off a little bit at a time. Stop cutting as soon as you notice a change. The next clipping may literally cut to the quick. With the soft, speckled nail, the closer you get to the quick, the more you will see a shiny black bull's-eye. Stop cutting when you see it.

Some dogs hold still better and accept the nails being worked on when a grinder is used. These come in various sizes and make anywhere from a low sound to a quite loud sound. One of the better ones is the Mighty Mite from Dremel. It is battery operated and has two speeds. It is usually less expensive than the grinders sold in pet stores or dog supply catalogs. The most important part about using a grinder is to NOT hold the sandpaper wheel against the toe. Gently touch and shape the toenail as the small wheel spins. The heat from the grinder can be transferred to the dog's nail and cause him some discomfort. Using the grinder about once a week will actually help make the "quick" recede. Thus, you can have a shorter nail. Be especially careful of using a grinder with long-haired breeds of dogs! The hair on their feet can get wrapped up in the revolving grinder and cause pain. After that, Spike probably will not let you near him again with a grinder in your hand. If you have a long-haired breed, wet the foot before using a grinder. This will keep the hair away from the rotating head. You can also use panty hose or "knee highs." Cut the top off the panty hose if you don't have any knee highs and put it on Spike's foot. Pull it up tight enough for his nails to go through the hose. Now you can use the grinder without fear of catching any of his hair in the machine.

If you cut a toenail too short, there are commercially prepared solutions to help stop the bleeding. "Qwik Stop" is a powder that can be put on the cut portion of the toenail to stop the bleeding. It is worth the price, as it will last almost for the life of a dog. Styptic pencils will stop the bleeding, but the dog will feel some discomfort. You can scrape the bleeding nail across candle wax or a bar of Ivory soap to stop the bleeding. If it is not bleeding much, try flour or cornstarch to stem the seepage. Sometimes a piece from a brown paper bag will work.

When cutting toenails, start with the back feet first; most dogs are not as upset with those being cut as they are with their front nails being done. Even though most nails on the back feet are worn down more than the front feet, it is a good way for you to gain confidence in cutting the nails and for the dog to learn that it is okay. It is best to try and cut nails when the dog is totally tired out and resting. If you have someone to help you, have them feed Spike tasty treats while you clip the nails. Quit *before* he starts to get upset or tries to pull his foot away from you. Even if you only cut one toenail a day, if you keep it positive, you will eventually be able to cut the nails on all four feet in one setting.

You could physically hold Spike down and either cut his nails or have someone else cut them. In a few months, Spike may allow this to happen *without* trying to bite at you.

Again, easy does it in the beginning. Set the stage for the way you want Spike to respond to you when you do things to him.

Bathing

Allow Spike to become accustomed to the bathtub BEFORE you give him a bath. It is better to put up with a smelly Spike than it is to put him in the tub and give him a bath and scare him. Put Spike in the tub and give him a treat, play tug with him, give him a massage, even let him eat a meal in the tub. When Spike is displaying positive experiences with the tub, add a little LUKE-WARM water to the tub. Encourage him to play in it, splash some water on him, use a plastic cup and pour some water over him, always being friendly and positive in YOUR manner. Get him used to you applying Vaseline or mineral oil into the lower lid of his eye. Spike will need this to protect his eyes against stinging from the shampoo. If you decide to wash Spike outside with the garden hose, have someone with you to take his attention off what you are doing. Have the other person give him treats, talk to him, play a little with him. If at any time, Spike becomes leery of the bathing process, give him a break and let him play or run around. If you are going to hose Spike off outside, make sure you have warm water ready in a bucket for the final rinse so that he won't become too chilled.

Each breed has varying degrees of natural coat oil. These oils collect and keep the dirt. Dogs need to be bathed whenever they are dirty or smell. (Even a short-haired breed may need weekly shampoos if he has skin allergies.) If your family seems to be having one cold after another and you are all patting the dog, give him a bath whether he is due for one or not. The coat oils can be holding onto particles of the cold or flu virus.

Before bathing Spike, comb him out to get rid of any mats you encounter. Pitch, grease, or chewing gum on Spike's coat can be removed with mineral oil or a sugar and water solution. Never use turpentine! It is flammable and causes the coat to be overly dry and brittle.

What you bathe Spike in is important, since you do not want to strip the coat oils away. It should be a shampoo made only for dogs. Some shampoos made for dogs and used on cats can have an adverse effect so be sure to read the label carefully. Unless he has an overly oily coat, an overly dry coat, or other skin problems, a regular cleaning shampoo will work well. Any skin problems should be checked by a vet; use whatever he/she recommends for bathing Spike. Be careful not to get irritating soap in the ears and eyes. Protect the eyes with Vaseline or mineral oil and put cotton balls in the ears. (Remember to remove these when you are done!) Use an old washcloth to clean the face. Really rinse the dog well. Any soap residue left behind can cause skin irritations and itching.

Shampoos that have an insecticide added to them to help with flea or tick control should not be used on young puppies. Read the label carefully before using any such products. Remember to always rinse Spike really well.

If Spike spends a lot of time outside or is bathed frequently, he may need to have a coat conditioner applied every few weeks. This should be a conditioner made for dogs. It will help reduce the number of split ends, keep his coat from fading in the summer, reduce itching, and help prevent mats. Some coat conditioners stay in for a week at a time and then need to be rinsed out. Others you can let sit for a few minutes and then rinse out. This type of coat conditioner lasts for a week or two, depending on how dirty the dog gets, his type of coat, how much time he spends outside.

Ear and Teeth Care

You may need to dry out the inside of Spike's ears after he goes swimming. Gently put a cotton ball into the ear canal as far as you can reach and then pull it back out.

Some breeds need to have the hair in their ears plucked out to prevent bacteria from building up and causing an ear infection. It is difficult to clean a dog's ears with Q-tips because the ear canal is shaped like the letter *L*. When you put a Q-tip into the ear, you actually push the dirt down into the ear beyond your reach. This may cause an ear infection. Putting a little mineral oil on the end of a Q-tip and cleaning the part of the ear that you can see would be okay. Use cotton balls to gently reach into the dog's ear and wipe out any dirt or earwax that has built up in the ear canal. When using a liquid to clean a dog's ears, squirt just a little into the ear canal. Massage the base of the ear; that will help loosen any wax. With the cotton, wipe out what you can reach. Keep massaging the base of the ear and the canal in an upward motion, and you will help bring up more wax and dirt from the bottom of the ear canal. Most dogs do fine with very little ear cleaning. Before putting anything other than mineral oil in your dog's ears, check with your veterinarian. If Spike has an ear problem, the vet will prescribe the correct type of ointment to use.

Dogs with a good deal of hair around the outside of the ear and on the inside of the earflap may need to be shaved periodically. If air cannot circulate around the ear to dry it, the area will become a breeding ground for bacteria, resulting in an ear infection. Certain breeds, such as the poodle, need to have the hair inside their ears plucked out. Otherwise, the hair keeps the ear canal moist and allows bacteria to grow, causing an ear infection.

If Spike has long ears, you may want to get a "snood" for him. This goes over the top of Spike's head and ears, keeping them out of the way of his dinner. This way, you do not have to wash the ends of Spike's ears at the end of every meal. If Spike has fairly long hair on his legs and you want to give him a rawhide bone or something else to chew on that might get stuck on the leg hair, consider using an old sock that has had the toe cut out. Slide this sock up Spike's legs and let him have his chew toy. Once he is done, take the sock off. You will not have to spend any extra time grooming him.

Brushing your dog's teeth is one way to help fight bad breath and cut down on the expense of having the vet put Spike under general anesthesia to clean and polish his teeth. Eating dry dog food or biscuits is not enough. In order to avoid gum disease, plaque needs to be removed.

Try using an old washcloth wrapped around your finger. Get Spike used to your sliding it in his mouth before putting any dog toothpaste on it. Human toothpaste or baking soda tastes terrible to most dogs, and they will try to avoid you when they see you with a toothbrush or rag. Human toothpaste could also make Spike sick. Dog toothpaste comes in flavors he likes (e.g., chicken, beef, and liver). Brush his teeth when the house is quiet and he is tired. You will have more success. Giving him a treat or playtime afterward will certainly help your cause.

Dogs like to roll in foul smelling matter. This helps to disguise their real odor so that they can creep up on unsuspecting animals. Even though most dogs don't hunt for their food anymore, this habit is very ingrained in their memory banks. Some dogs even seem to go out of their way to get dirty again as soon as they have been given a bath. Maybe you need to think about changing the shampoo you are bathing Spike in.

Besides bathing and grooming Spike on a regular basis to have him look and smell clean, it is a time for you to check him out for any lumps, bumps, or tumors that were not there the last time you felt him all over.

Fleas and Ticks

Nothing man has invented to date can kill an entire flea population. However, there are products on the market that will stop flea eggs from hatching, render female fleas sterile, or kill the infant flea before it has a chance to grow and reproduce. Check with your vet about products that are best for your situation. Does your dog go swimming? How many other animals are in the family? Any cats? Check out what is best for you to use—dips, shampoos, sprays, powders, and so on. Don't forget to use something on the house, yard, and especially his dog bed.

Flea and tick preparations that you purchase from your vet may be a little more expensive than those from the grocery or drugstore, but the ingredients are stronger because they have been checked out by the FDA for sale by a licensed vet. Grocery and drugstore brands do not have the quality control; therefore, they have a lower price but a weaker concentration and less effectiveness.

Chapter 18

Nutrition

Good nutrition is the foundation for the future health of Spike. More studies are showing that proper nutrition may decrease the incidence or stop the growth of cancer, may reduce the risk of heart or kidney problems, and may reduce the risk of a gastric torsion, allowing Spike to live a longer and healthier life.

Unless your dog spends 90 percent of his time outside during the winter, is heavily exercised (more than four miles a day), or is a guard, herding, or show dog, he does not need a high protein diet. Feeding the average house dog such a diet tends to make him hyper and on edge. Behavior problems may result; animals tend to become destructive in the house as they try to burn off the higher protein and fat diet.

Dogs should eat plain, wholesome food. They need a little variety in their food, but a lot may lead to diarrhea or chronic intestinal problems. Dogs do see some colors, but that is not why they like one food over another. Dogs like foods that feel good in their mouths and have enough fat to entice them to eat. Food colorings, sugar, nitrates, nitrites, and some preservatives tend to make some dogs hyperactive. It is best to avoid these ingredients when choosing a diet. They are there for the humans only, as gimmicks to buy the food. Spike does not need any of these extras. In fact, these additives may cause Spike to have a Jekyll and Hyde personality!

Shapes, gravies, and flavors are designed to sell us the dog food. The dog will eat anything if hungry enough. But is it the right food for him? Some shapes make dogs cough more because the food irritates the lining of the throat as they swallow it. Some dogs cannot tolerate the gravy; others do not care for certain flavors. The wrong food can result in diarrhea or not wanting to eat.

Be careful or you could encourage Spike to become a fussy eater. If he chooses to pick at a meal or skip a meal or two and you immediately head out to get him a different bag of food, you may be teaching Spike to be a picky eater. For example, he will eat one food for a few weeks and than start to pick and leave meals. Then you bring home another new food, and the cycle starts again. Or he may become bored with his food and, by picking at it, get you to bring home a new food almost every month. A healthy dog will not starve himself to death; he'll just get a little thinner until he decides to eat what is put before him.

Feeding Schedules

Puppies of almost any breed need to be fed three times a day until they are about five to six months of age. Spike will let you know when it is time to take a meal away: He may not finish a meal, he may be slow to eat, or he may not even approach the bowl. Don't reduce the number of feedings before Spike is ready, or he may become more mouthy and nippy.

Large/giant breed puppies should eat adult dog food, rather than puppy food, the first year of life! In fact, orthopedic specialists have agreed that feeding large/giant breed puppies (or puppies with lots of bone mass) puppy food after twenty weeks of age is unnecessary and may increase the pup's chances of hip dysplasia or other joint problems. A puppy fed adult dog food will attain his full growth and weight; he just may take a few more months to do so.

The smaller breeds of dogs have faster metabolisms than the larger breeds of dogs. Therefore, pound for pound, puppies of the smaller breeds need to eat even more often than puppies of the larger breeds. The larger breed puppy can hold more food at one time than the smaller breed puppy. So giving the smaller puppy three to five meals a day would be beneficial to that puppy, rather than the usual two to three meals a day for the larger breed pup.

Letting a pup self-feed, by leaving the food dish down and full all day, may lead to behavior problems in the future:

1. Spike will tend to guard the house or the area near his food with growling or aggression.
2. He will not think he owes his existence to anyone, because every time he wants to eat, there is always food.

3. Without regular meals, bowel function is not predictable, and house-training is more complicated.

4. Pups that self-feed do not seem to gain weight as easily as their littermates. They seem to need food presented at intervals, which is nature's way.

5. Pups of large breeds have a higher incident of hip dysplasia when self-fed.

Since most dogs are chow hounds, they do better with two meals a day. How much you feed per meal depends on the dog and his activity level. Ideally you should be able to feel Spike's ribs but not see them. If you have to dig your fingers into Spike's flesh to feel his ribs, he is overweight. Being overweight ages a dog faster, increases wear and tear to his joints, and adds stress to his overall condition. Giant breeds of dogs should be fed three to four meals a day to reduce their risk of a gastric torsion or bloat. Elevating their food bowl is also beneficial. Some meat-based brands of food may aggravate arthritic conditions. If Spike seems to be more arthritic than you think he should be at his age, try changing his type of dog food. If Spike is eating a beef-based food, try a chicken-based food. If on a chicken-based food, try beef or lamb. It may take a few months before you notice an improvement.

If Spike is a very fast eater, he may not feel that he has eaten enough and may go looking for snacks. A puppy that eats very fast may also nip and mouth more. To slow down a fast eater, place two *large* rocks (the size of your fist) in the food dish. Make sure the rocks are too large for Spike to swallow. If you only put one rock in, Spike will chase the food around the rock and eat almost as fast as before. Two large rocks force Spike to work longer to pick up the nuggets, and as a result, his meal lasts longer, and he feels more satisfied. If you have just one dog, scatter his food over the kitchen floor. That will certainly stop Spike from gulping large amounts of food at a time. Scattering his food on a large cookie sheet may suffice if this is not your idea of a great floor washing technique.

Choosing a Dog Food

Read food labels. Choose a good quality, well-balanced, well-known brand that does not contain additives such as nitrates, caramel, and food coloring. The key to choosing a good diet are the terms *completely balanced* or *meets or exceeds NRC (National Research Council) requirements* or *tested by AAFCO (Association of American Feed Control Officials) feeding trials.* The phrase *100 percent complete nutrition* only means that it is edible. Well, so are chicken feathers! It does not necessarily mean that the food is a balanced diet or that it will sustain the dog in all stages of his life.

The guidelines on the bags of food are there as examples. If you have to feed eight cups of food a day to your sixty-pound dog to get all his daily nutritional requirements, you may want to consider another brand of dog food. Grocery and feed-store brands of dog food do not undergo the same quality control that the more expensive brands do. That is why the expensive brands are more expensive. The grocery or feed-store brand can change ingredients without having to change the label. Your dog might do okay being fed from one bag, but the next bag might cause diarrhea or vomiting, or he may just turn his nose up at it.

Generic brands of dog food are cheaper to buy. But in the long run, they may cost you more; they often cause skin or bone problems.

The concentrated brands of food that you buy from a pet store or vet's office are of better quality. Concentrated diets have more nutrients packed in a smaller volume; thus fewer cups of food are needed. The added advantage is that Spike produces less stool because the body utilizes the food better. Cleaning the yard is faster and easier! With these concentrated brands, you need to reduce the amount of food you feed Spike. Read the directions. With the concentrated diets that tend to be quite rich, if too much is fed at once, Spike may end up with diarrhea. But if you are trying to get Spike to gain weight, some of these diets won't work unless you're careful to increase the food by increasing the number of meals to avoid diarrhea. If Spike is otherwise doing well on the food and you do not want to change it, try another version to see if he gains weight. If Spike is eating Nature's Recipe Lamb and Rice, try Nature's Recipe Lamb, Rice, and Barley or Nature's Recipe Chicken and Rice. Changing to another variety of food made by the same company may be all that is necessary for Spike to gain some weight.

Dry Dog Food

Dry dog food is the most inexpensive way to feed Spike, even when purchasing the more expensive brand. Adding a little **hot** water and letting it cool down before feeding Spike can be of value. Adding cool water can encourage loose stools. The hot water kills whatever bacteria might be present on the food, encouraging firm stools. Water added to dry food also helps keep the dog from choking or coughing on the "fines"—these are tiny pieces of food that are rubbed off in the bag as the nuggets rub against each other.

Beware of foods that state they are "naturally preserved" and have a shelf life of six months to a year. Vitamin E goes rancid after nine weeks and vitamin C won't preserve the food for an entire year! Dog food companies that buy meat with preservatives already in it do not have to state that on their label. Since they did not add the preservative, they don't have to mention it.

There is quite a bit of controversy about the kind and amount of preservatives used in dog food. You will find preservatives in dry, canned, and semimoist food. BHA and BHT have been taken out of human food because they can strip the myelin off nerves and cause schizophrenia. They have also been labeled as a carcinogen. Ethoxiquin is said to be related to a number of health problems (e.g., fertility problems in females, low-birth weight and other complications in newborns, skin problems, and cancer). This is not included to scare you but to make you aware that even some of the most expensive brands have all three types of preservative in their food. If it has been deemed unsafe for humans, why is it safe for animals? They have the same health issues as we do.

There are a few exceptions to this. Wysong, Solid Gold, Pet Guard, Precise, and Innova either vacuum pack their food or make it when an order comes in; thus, it does not sit for long periods in a storehouse. These foods are made from high-quality ingredients with no extra frills. The food contains only the necessary ingredients. Bil-Jac is another dog food company that makes food and immediately freezes it. There are no preservatives added to the food. This Midwest company has retailers all the way to the East Coast. Unfortunately, the frozen variety of their food is still not available in the West.

Dry food may not be every dog's dream of the ideal diet, but few of us have the time or knowledge to cook for our dogs. No dog will starve himself to death if he is healthy. Dogs that do not want to eat dry dog food are waiting to see what you will bring home next to tempt their palate.

Proper storage of dry dog food is important. Always leave the food in the bag and store it away from heat, light, and strong odors. Emptying it into a plastic container will allow formaldehyde to seep into the food. However, if you buy a forty-pound bag for one dog and it stays open and uncovered for a month or more, it may turn rancid. For one large dog or a few small dogs, a twenty-pound bag is best, though a little more costly for you. The best storage method is to leave the food in the bag and place the entire bag in a container with a tight-fitting lid.

Canned Food

Canned food is one of the most expensive ways to feed your dog, if that is all you feed him. Adding a quarter to a third of a large can to your dog's dry food will encourage him to eat better, and it will not be as expensive. Canned food is NOT made up of prime cuts of meat. Rather it is made up of the parts of the animal that are not fit for human consumption. Or it could be meat that normally would have been okay for a human to eat but has already started to spoil or rot.

It only takes a tenth of a percent of liver in the can to be called "liver stew"! You are mostly paying for 70 percent water, a label, and the can. The rest of the contents is "filler"—edible but not very nutritious.

Most of the canned food from pet stores, vet offices, and better boarding kennels is made up of better quality ingredients. Again, you will pay more for better food. Remember, prescription diets for specific health conditions are to be fed to Spike ONLY upon advice from your veterinarian.

If you are adding canned food to Spike's dry meal, put the canned food in the dish first or mix the two together. This way, Spike will not be able to pick out the canned food and leave the rest.

Semimoist Foods

Semimoist food has more sugar, salt, and preservatives then any other dog food on the market. Most of these ingredients can cause a dog to be hyperactive or moody. It comes in a variety of shapes and sizes—like hamburg or stew meat. This is also the most costly way to feed a large dog. An occasional piece as a treat might be okay; anything more tends to be unhealthy.

Table Scraps, Homemade Food, and Supplements

Food scraps from the table can be added to Spike's dish in place of canned food. Table/food scraps, canned horse meat, and a brand or two of mixed meat and grain were the only dog foods available till the 1940s. Dry dog food did not really appear until the 1950s! Watch what you give Spike though. Gravies, skin, bones, pork, and rich foods do not sit well with Spike. In fact, they can cause irreversible problems. Onions, cooked or raw, should never be fed to dogs or cats (they can cause anemia).

If you want to make your own food for Spike, please read a lot of books on the subject (you will find some listed in the bibliography) so that you are sure to give him all the nutrients he needs. Offering Spike a variety of veggies, meats, and carbos is one way to assure yourself that he is getting all the nutrients that he needs. It can and has been done, and the owners have had healthy dogs with great skin, coat, eyes, teeth, and so on, and no lumps or bumps until really older age. It does take time, money, and research in the beginning to determine the right ingredients, make the food, store it, and find out where to get the most inexpensive, good quality products. In the long run, if you own one to three dogs, it will not cost you any more to make your own dog food than if you bought the most expensive brand on the market. Most breeders and people who have had dogs for years seldom keep their dogs on the same dry food for more than five years. It follows that they are not sure their dogs are receiving all that they should, so they switch foods every five years. Some even have two to three brands of dry dog food that they rotate and feed their dogs. Dry dog foods may not be the total answer for you, nor may making your own dog food. Again, you need to do what is right for you, depending on the time you have and your dog. Even the most expensive brand of food is not right for all dogs. If a dog's body cannot absorb the nutrients in a particular brand, then what good is it? By making your own food and having a variety of carbos, veggies, and meats, you know Spike is getting all that he needs and more.

Supplementing Spike's meal with yogurt (brands with acidophilus cultures is best), cottage cheese, and the occasional cooked egg will add "friendly" bacteria to his intestinal tract and shine to his coat. Caution: Dogs cannot digest or utilize the nutrients from uncooked egg whites.

Whether supplementing with fresh foods, veggies, yogurt, or making your own food, you need to be able to know what, if any, foods Spike is allergic to. In the beginning, put a veggie like green beans through the food processor on high until it is shredded as much as possible. Just add a tablespoon to his regular food for one meal. Now observe Spike for four days. Does he rub his head along the floor/furniture, shake his head, paw at his face, break out in little bumps, or have a change in the consistency of his stool? Are the insides of his ears warmer and pinker? If not, then he is probably not allergic to green beans. Now try another veggie. Carrots have a lot of cellulose and must be put either through a juicer or a food processor until the pieces are as small as possible. (You may still see particles of carrots in Spike's stool.) Once you know what he can and can't eat, you can make up enough food for a week at a time. Some dogs who have food allergies do much better on homemade diets. Even some of the foods that they are usually allergic to, when prepared fresh, are tolerable.

Supplementing with extra vitamins/mineral tablets or a single vitamin should be discussed with your veterinarian. If you overdo one or two vitamins or minerals, it throws off the balance, and over a period of time the dog could actually become vitamin deficient, resulting in growth or bone formation problems. One dog food company added eight times the recommended daily requirements for all vitamins and minerals except vitamins A and D. Those were sixteen times higher than recommended. Black-haired dogs turned bronze, and several grayish dogs turned a shade of pink! Over a long period of time, what else might have gone wrong with the dog?

Treats

Dog biscuits and other type treats are okay as a *treat*. That means you give a tiny piece (about as big as your thumbnail to the average forty-five-pound dog) as a treat. Anything more becomes a meal. Too many treats and Spike starts to put on weight. So, if you really want to give him a piece of your donut, a small piece is sufficient, not half of the donut. Treats should be without color (color can cause hyperactivity) and something the dog can chew easily.

Do not give Spike chocolate or onions! Chocolate may cause seizures and/or death. Onions, as mentioned earlier, may cause Spike to become anemic. There are "chocolate" treats for dogs, BUT they are made with carob, not real chocolate, and are safe for Spike.

How to Change Foods

Changing from one brand of dry dog food to another may cause Spike to have diarrhea. To avoid this problem, change gradually. Buy the new brand while you still have some of the old brand left. Mix one part new food with three parts old food for at least two days. If Spike does not have loose stools or diarrhea, mix equal amounts of new food and old food for at least two days. If Spike is still okay, mix three parts new food with one part old food for at least two days. If he is still okay, give Spike a few days on just the new food. How is he doing? Some dogs may not be able to tolerate a change from a chicken-based diet to one of beef or lamb and vice versa. If the new food is going right through Spike (loose stools) he is unable to absorb the nutrients. Regardless of how great the quality is or how much you paid for it, the food will not work for Spike.

If Spike has any loose stools during the changeover from one food to another, go back to the ratio in which he still had formed stools. You may need to go more slowly with the addition of new food. Check the date on the bag of food; it may be too old. Where has it been stored? If left open too long, it will start to turn rancid. In the end, this may not be a food that is agreeable to Spike.

In some instances when you change diets on Spike, he may lose most of his coat. This is normal; within a month or so an even better looking coat start, to regrow. If the new coat takes longer than two months to start to reappear or it is of poorer quality than it used to be, maybe the new diet is not agreeing with Spike.

If Spike has diarrhea at any time, consult with his veterinarian to see what steps you should take. Sometimes, simply withholding food and water for twenty-four hours is all that is necessary. Sometimes, the food may be bad (e.g., moldy or too old). Maybe during a change of foods, you took only two to three days to have Spike adjust to the new food instead of seven days. Sometimes feeding him boiled hamburger and rice will help—do this only if Spike is acting his normal self. He should be fine after a few days. Then add this mixture to his old food for a few days to help the change back to his normal food.

Stool Eating

While it may seem inappropriate to mention coprophagy (stool eating) in this section, a number of dogs will eat their own or other's poop for a number of reasons:

1. Stool eating in pups/dogs may indicate a disease that impairs normal digestion of food. It is best to have a stool-eating dog examined by a veterinarian for possible health problems.
2. Overfeeding by feeding the dog's daily rations in a single meal may be the culprit. Because the systems of some dogs cannot fully digest the nutrients in a single meal, many of the nutrients are passed in the stool. Spike, later feeling the lack of these nutrients, goes out and eats his

stool. Changing to two meals a day will help. You may also need to change the brand of food.

3. Some dogs learn to eat their stool from watching their owners pick it up. You want a clean yard, and they want a job. So they help. Some house-soiling dogs will eat their stool to hide the evidence, thereby avoiding punishment.

4. A lot of dogs learn to eat their stool during the winter time when it is frozen. It seems that they begin by playing with it—tossing it into the air and catching it. Then some of it slides down their throat. Once tasted, most of them start to hunt out the stool and consume it.

To keep Spike from starting this bad habit, pick up the stools when he is not out there with you, but leave some and douse them with Tabasco. Sometimes adding pineapple juice or thawed spinach to his food will change the enzyme structure, and Spike will not want to eat the stool. There are products available such as a powder called Forbid that does the same thing and works on some dogs. If you have several dogs, this can become costly. Again, you may want to change your dog's food to see if that helps. Another approach is to teach Spike the command "Leave It." After he understands the command, use it when he approaches a stool. If he leaves it alone on the first command, offer him a treat. He may seek out every stool just to get your attention and a treat, but that is much more acceptable than eating stool!

Chapter 19

Seasonal Dangers

Hot Weather

Hot days are NOT the time to take Spike with you when you do your errands. On an eighty degree day, the inside of your car will reach one-hundred degrees in less then fifteen minutes—and that's with all the windows down! In twenty minutes, Spike could be having heatstroke and dying. Rule of thumb: If the sky is clear with no clouds and it is sixty-five degrees by 10 A.M., it will become too warm for Spike to be in the car. And contrary to what you might think, dogs traveling in the back of a pickup, despite the breeze, can get overheated from the lack of shade. (See the chapter entitled "Traveling with Spike" for more detailed information.)

Spike can only cool himself off by panting; he cannot sweat. The pads of his feet may sweat slightly, but not enough to cool him off. He can dehydrate rapidly doing a lot of panting, so make sure he always has plenty of fresh, cool water available.

If Spike spends a fair amount of time outside, he should have a child's wading pool to cool off in. This will need to be cleaned periodically, or it will become a breeding ground for mosquitoes. And there **MUST** be part of the yard where he can find shade and dig in the ground to find a cool spot.

Even when inside, a dog can get heatstroke if the house is too warm. Those at high risk are the breeds with pushed-in noses, older dogs, dogs that have respiratory problems, and dogs that bark too much (they overheat easily in hot weather). Keep him cool and quiet on those hot days by putting him in the coolest place in the house, providing fresh water, and perhaps hosing him down. Don't just mist Spike—the heat will evaporate the mist on his coat, generating more heat for him. Wet him down entirely, all the way through his coat to his skin. Even putting him in his crate with ice cubes under him can be a big help. It will also confine him so that he does not get everything all wet while he dries. Consider putting a fan near Spike on those extremely warm days, but be sure it is out of his reach.

If Spike has a temperature of 103.5 degrees during hot weather or when he is slightly excited, it is normal. Anything higher SHOULD be referred to the vet for advice immediately! (You will need a regular rectal thermometer to find out Spike's temp. Put a little Vaseline, mineral oil, butter, or soap to help grease the end so it will slide into Spike easier with less fuss from him. Ear and digital thermometers have not been very successful with animals yet.)

During the summer months, do not walk your dog on lawns treated with lawn chemicals or that have regular maintenance by lawn care professionals (they usually place little flags along the edges of the grass for twenty-four hours after the lawn has been treated to alert you). The National Cancer Institute reports that dogs and humans who live in or near homes whose yards are routinely treated have twice the risk of lymphatic cancer. That seems like a good reason not to need to have the best lawn in the neighborhood. Maybe you can convince neighbors who have used these chemicals in the past that they shouldn't use them any more. This is especially true if you have well water.

Watch for broken bottles, tin cans, sharp objects, and things you would rather Spike did not put into his mouth or walk on during your walk. Shoulders of roads and edges of ponds, streams, and lakes seem to have more than their share of such things. Taking Spike for a nice swim on a warm day can end up with a visit to the vet with a badly cut foot pad, if you are not alert to this kind of litter.

Cold Weather

In the winter, clean off your dog's feet if he has been out walking in the sand/salt mixture used in the snowbelt area. Even most of the commercial deicers on the market that you can use around your home are not safe for animals. Licking this off his feet can cause anything from an upset stomach to more serious problems.

To clean off Spike's feet, fill an old plastic dishpan with hot water (before you head out for your walk). The water will be lukewarm by the time you return. You might only be able to do a foot at a time or the front end and then the back end. You could also wipe Spike's feet with a few old towels soaked with warm water.

Anytime of the year, but especially during the winter, watch out for antifreeze. It has a sweet smell and taste that makes dogs and kids want to drink it. It only takes a teaspoonful to kill small dogs and cats. If you suspect Spike has licked some antifreeze, contact your veterinarian IMMEDIATELY! There is at least one brand of antifreeze on the market that is not attractive to kids and animals.

Watch out for seemingly frozen ponds and lakes. In some areas—such as over moving water or under bridges—the ice will not be as thick and you or your dog can fall through. Until you know for sure that the ice is safe enough to hold you, it is wiser to keep Spike off it too.

In snow country, when it is dry and very cold, with snow on the ground, most dogs have a difficult time walking because the pads on their feet get cold. Spike will suddenly act like he doesn't know which foot to lift up. When this happens, it is usually too cold to take him for a walk. Some dogs with sweaty pads may even stick to ice or really hard snow. Dogs with hair between their toes get snowballs in those places. These balls can become as hard as a rock and make walking difficult and painful for Spike. Try stopping Spike periodically on the walk and cleaning out between his toes. Some people have better results by trimming the hair between his toes. Others spray Pam on Spike's feet (outside in the yard) before going for a walk to reduce ice buildup between the toes. Ask friends what they do for their dogs. Some people even put on doggie boots to protect their dog's feet. It takes a while for Spike to become used to these and not rip them off or shake them off. They work okay in snow but do not allow much traction on ice.

If Spike is going to stay outside in any season, but especially during the winter, he **must** have some shelter to go to in case it turns colder or starts to snow before you get home. Dogs that are outside a fair amount of the day need A LOT more food than a house dog. It takes calories to stay warm. A long walk during the winter calls for more food to keep Spike warm than a walk during the warmer months. Make sure that his shelter opening does not face north or northwest, since more wind will get in. His shelter should also be elevated off the ground, regardless of the season. Being off the ground will keep it dry during the rain and warmer when it is cold. There should also be a flap or covering over the opening so that when Spike is in the doghouse, the warmth from his body is retained in the shelter. Water will freeze quickly when left outside. There are gadgets available from pet supply catalogs and farm supply stores that you plug into an electrical outlet and then submerge into the water bucket or dish to keep the water from freezing. However, some can short circuit and give Spike a shock when he tries to get a drink of water. It's best to check on the water bowl as often as possible. If it is so cold that the water freezes in an hour or two, Spike should not be outside. It is way too cold for him!

Fleas, Ticks, and Other Pests

Fleas and ticks are out and about from spring to fall. In some parts of the country, they are out year-round. Fleas spend the majority of their time on the animal. Taking care of Spike (and especially any cats in the family) will help, but you will still need to take care of the house (and the yard if there are year-round problems). If you do not take care of the house and grounds, Spike will keep getting fleas. Do not allow flea infestations to go unchecked, or you or your family will be their next meal. A dog allergic to flea bites can itch for twenty-four hours from just one bite. A flea lives an average of nine months. In that time, one male and one female flea can be responsible for 222 trillion eggs! (this is not a misprint.) Flea Buster is a fine powder-type product that may be sprinkled around the doorways, floors, and rugs of your house. You leave it down for twenty-four hours and then vacuum it up. This powder dries up a flea egg, making it impossible for it to hatch. Thus, the population eventually dies down or out completely. You might want to restrict Spike's access to those areas. While it is safe for him to walk on this powder, you might not want him to lick it off his feet. A few dogs have reacted to it, but it is generally extremely safe.

Ticks can carry Lyme disease (though not all deer ticks do) and Rocky Mountain Spotted Fever. You might want to wear rubber gloves when removing a tick from an animal or yourself. Grasp the tick firmly with either tweezers or your fingers, as close to the head end of the tick as you can. With a long-haired breed of dog, wet the hair around the tick to keep the hair out of the way. Because ticks have mouth parts like a crab, it is difficult to get the mouth part out. But with a quick twist pull, you should be able to pop the tick head and all off. If the mouth is left behind, it will come out in due time. A tick injects an anticoagulant under the dog's skin in order to suck his blood. Some dogs have a reaction to this anticoagulant and will have a bump in that spot for up to a month. It is very similar how we react to a mosquito bite.

Do not use a flame of any kind to try and get the tick to withdraw his head! It does not usually work and in most cases, you end up burning or scorching Spike. And don't use a match that has just been lit and then blown out. It is still too hot to put near Spike's skin or coat.

Putting Vaseline on the tick will cause him to smother, but it could take quite a while before the dead tick falls off. And on a long-haired breed of dog, the Vaseline can get wiped off all over your furniture.

Flushing the tick down the toilet will not kill it. If you have a septic system and leach field, the tick will probably end up in your warm, moist leach field, a perfect breeding ground for a tick. If you are going to squash the tick, make sure it is wrapped up in something first; it makes less of a mess. Also squishing the tick will release bacteria, so if you do kill the tick this way, make sure he is between several layers of tissue. Another method is to put the tick in a jar with mineral oil or Vaseline and smother him; alcohol will work also.

If you want to clean up the skin where the tick was attached, use plain lukewarm water first. Than you can use a little hydrogen peroxide or alcohol. Both will sting the open wound. Blot the area and leave it open to scab over. Putting Vaseline or the like on the area will only slow down healing. And the more you put on it, the more Spike will be apt to either lick, chew, or rub off.

When you take Spike in the car to go someplace for a walk, you don't want him bringing any extra critters back to the house. So either spray him with flea and/or tick spray before you leave the house or comb him before letting him back in the car. Some sprays are in a more concentrated form, like mousse. These cannot be applied every day but will last a week or more, depending on whether Spike gets wet or not.

Mosquitoes in many parts of the United States and Canada carry heartworm. Check with your veterinarian to see if you need to put Spike on heartworm prevention. This is a life-threatening disease. And there are rare incidences of cats and humans getting heartworm. Even if you have Spike on a year-round preventative, he still should be blood checked yearly (some vets are now allowing Spike to go two years before being tested; you do what feels right to you). If your batch of medication was made without the primary preventive ingredient, Spike could be positive for heartworm. The chances are extremely slim of that ever happening, but we do not live in a perfect world. "Better safe than sorry" is the way to go.

Choices of heartworm medication range from daily tablets, daily liquid, and at least two varieties of once-a-month tablets or chewables. Go over the choices with your vet and choose the one right for Spike, not just what is more convenient. There are pros and cons to all the medications. If you are going to use a daily heartworm preventative, be sure to have him checked *before* giving him the medication! If Spike is positive for heartworm, the strong reaction of the daily medication can kill him. Heartworm medication is based on Spike's weight. If he is growing, you may need to have him weighed monthly to make sure he is getting enough of the preventative. Even after he is an adult, a gain in weight would call for a higher dose.

Parasites are more active during the warmer months. So have your vet check a stool sample from Spike for worms. In the southern part of the United States, it is unhealthy to go barefoot in areas frequented by dogs because the worm larvae can get into tiny cuts in a human foot and set up housekeeping.

Some signs of Spike having worms might be scooting on his fanny (this could indicate anal gland problems also), diarrhea, dull coat, lethargy, and so on.

If Spike has been drinking out of puddles of water, slow flowing streams, ponds, or lakes, he could have Giardia. This is not a parasite, rather it is a protozoa. It will not show up in stool samples. Usually it is found by doing a direct smear—taking a Q-tip, inserting it into the dog's rectum, and putting it directly onto a microscope slide. Symptoms are intermittent diarrhea. It is treatable.

Spring, summer, and fall are the seasons for skunks and porcupines. It is best to take the dog to the vet if he gets involved with a porcupine. It is easier on the dog to be put under a general anesthetic (or sedation, depending on how many quills need to be pulled) to have the quills pulled. Also, the pain while having them pulled out could cause Spike to bite someone. Leaving the quills in overnight does not teach the dog to avoid the critter in the future. Usually it has the opposite effect; Spike will try to kill the next one he sees. Cutting the tip off the quill DOES NOT make it easier to pull it out. The opposite is true; it makes it harder to pull out, since the quill is softer and can break apart more easily.

If he gets sprayed by a skunk, protect his eyes and ears and give him a bath with regular pH-balanced shampoo; rinse well. Then make up a solution of one-half cup of Clorox and one gallon of water. Thoroughly wet him; use an old face cloth to do his face—this is where Spike usually gets most of the spray. Let the solution sit for a few minutes and then rinse really well! You may need to do his face and the front of his chest again, but it usually works great the first time—and does not leave him orange like tomato juice will. (Most everyone has bleach on hand, but not everyone has five gallons of tomato juice just waiting for when their dog gets sprayed by a skunk.) Other alternatives include (1) hydrogen peroxide mixed with water and shampoo and (2) a women's vinegar douche. These methods are okay for small dogs, but you would need quite a supply for a large dog. You could try just vinegar, either white or apple cider, if that is all you have on hand. Some pet shops and animal hospitals sell a product called Skunk Off. It is the only commercial product that I have found that works well.

In certain parts of the country, snakes, toads, and frogs can be poisonous. Also, beware of fire ants in the southern United States. Check around for snake clinics; they are run by knowledgeable people to train your dog to avoid being bitten by a snake. If new to the area, check with the local veterinarians to find out what critters are harmful to Spike.

Watch pups in the springtime; they love to chase and eat bumblebees and hornets. If you find out that Spike has an allergy to such stings, make sure you have something on hand in case of an emergency.

If Spike is bitten by a snake, hornet, bee, or wasp, the first thing to do is apply a cold compress or ice pack to the area and keep Spike calm. The more he moves around and the warmer the area bitten or stung, the more the venom travels. If you have someone with you, have him/her help keep Spike quiet and phone the animal hospital to see what to do next.

If you find any fire ants on Spike, hose him off as quickly as possible. If you managed to see that the ants were grouped in one place on Spike more than another, try to put cold compresses on that area. Again, phone the vet to see what else to do for Spike.

(For more detailed information about animal parasites, see the chapter entitled "Health and First Aid.")

Miscellaneous Hazards

Do you have any harmful plants, shrubs, or bushes that Spike can get to and ingest? You may want to consider putting a shrubbery fence around those plants that are suspect. The top part of the acorn nut (called a cap) is toxic to most dogs. Some have to eat a lot to have a problem; others need to eat only one or two before they start shivering, drooling, vomiting, and so on. Call the vet to see what to do next. If you do not have anything on hand to make Spike vomit, let the vet know; he may want you to come right in with Spike.

Mushrooms can have the same bad effect on some dogs. Be aware of any you may have in your backyard or other places where Spike goes for regular walks or runs when he is off the leash.

Watch your dog around fishing tackle boxes. Most dogs are too curious to stay away from a tackle box and will usually end up wearing a lure.

Every season of the year has its hazards. Watch where you put out the rodent, ant, cockroach, and spider poisons. D-con can kill Spike almost as fast as antifreeze can. Make sure you cover all paint, oil, and turpentine cans when Spike is around. Lead-based paints cause as many health problems with animals as they do with children. If Spike gets enough oil-based paint on him close to his skin, he may end up with severe health issues from it. Even some garden fertilizers and sprays can be toxic to Spike. All of these items should be stored either up out of Spike's reach or in a cabinet with a childproof lock.

Remember, good management will prevent most potential health hazards!

Chapter 20

Health and First Aid

Routine Health Care

Learn about the health of your dog. What is his normal temperature and heart rate? What are his normal exercise habits? How fast does he breathe when he is excited versus resting? What about his eating habits—is he a good eater or a slow eater? Any change from the ordinary is your signal to find out what's going on. Eyes should be clean, free of any discharge, and should have an alert expression. Ears should have a mild doggy odor about them and be clean.

Run your hands over your dog at least once a week. What is normal for your dog? Is this lump getting any larger? Is that a new lump? If and when you do find a lump, don't panic. Have the lump checked out by your vet, but unless it is bloody, it is not usually an emergency. Your vet will record the size and position of the lump and discuss with you what should be done next. You might want to make a note of the size and location for your records as well. Even young dogs under two years of age have had cancer. This is not meant to scare you; rather it is meant to inform you and encourage you to keep checking Spike.

Routine health care, regular checkups, and vaccinations are just as important for your dog as they are for you. This care should continue throughout his life. With routine checkups, your veterinarian can tell you when your dog's teeth need cleaning— before they fall out. He can check for and remove tumors before they become too large, and he can also make you aware of any changes in Spike's heart, lungs, eyes, or ears, or of any other health conditions. Having a routine blood profile done yearly, once Spike is over seven years of age, can detect potentially serious health problems like diabetes, liver and/or kidney disease, or anemia. Consider having a blood profile done twice a year on dogs over the age of ten. It is easier to treat problems when they are just beginning than when they have already damaged the dog's health. It is also less expensive in the long run. Whenever your dog is not acting himself, have him checked out or at least call your vet to see if he/she wants to see Spike.

Spaying/Neutering

Any dog not used for breeding should be neutered. Neutering your pets (male or female) will keep them healthier throughout their lifespan. Statistics prove that a female spayed before her first heat will have less of a chance of developing mammary tumors than an unspayed female. It is riskier to spay an older female—she may have a heart murmur, lung problems, and so on. There is no benefit in waiting until after her first heat cycle to have her spayed. She could get caught by the dog next door. Dogs bleed at the onset of their estrus cycle which lasts three weeks. Why put up with blood on your floors, carpets, furniture, and clothes if you are not going to breed her? Why put up with her whining and trying to get out all the time? Why put up with male dogs having fights in your yard? Why put up with dogs camping out on your doorstep, waiting to sneak into your house?

Males that are neutered have fewer prostate problems when older. Unneutered males tend to be more aggressive and dominant, tend to mark their territory more, and have more of a doggy odor about them. A neutered male will not want to wander as much or get into fights. A male dog can smell a female dog in season many miles away. Males have been known to jump out of second-story windows, dig under fences, and climb over six-foot chain-link fences to get to a female dog in season. Keeping an unneutered male around for a pet is like having a loaded gun in the house. What if he gets hit by a car while he is out? Does he have identification on so that you will be notified? What if he causes a car accident while he is out looking for a girlfriend? Can you afford the vet bill to patch him up and the lawsuit for causing the accident? What if he gets into a fenced-in backyard and mates with a purebred whose owner was not ready for a litter? They can sue you and usually win! It's not worth the risk; neutering is safer for him and your pocketbook.

Altering either sex does not necessarily make them fat, though some dogs will put on weight after being altered. Weight gain results from overeating, lack of exercise (his desire to roam is gone), and the loss of those active organs and hormones.

Neutering your pet is responsible pet ownership and will decrease the unwanted puppy population. *NEUTERED PETS MAKE BETTER PETS!*

Breeding

If you think you want to breed Spike, think again! Breeding dogs is a serious venture and should, in my opinion, be left to those who want to research all the potential problems of the breeds. (*Most* AKC recognized breeds have inherited health problems!) Intact males can easily become handling problems. If you have a female dog, there are many, many serious considerations to think about before you find yourself caring for a pregnant bitch. And despite popular myth, you don't need to wait for her first heat—and the potential for an accidental litter—to have your female pup spayed!

Anesthesia

If your dog ever needs an anesthetic, here are some tips on taking care of Spike the first day home: During recovery from an injury or surgery, most dogs will prefer to be left alone to sleep and may choose to skip a meal. He may be more wobbly than you realize and fall down a set of stairs or fall into the sharp corner of a table. He may need assistance to do simple tasks, such as going outside to go to the bathroom. Spike may cough for a few days due to a endotrachea tube having been fitted into his throat to administer the gas anesthesia. Some dogs may vomit, have diarrhea, or be constipated for a day or so after anesthesia. Most veterinarians will be happy to answer your questions about your pet's unusual behavior during recovery. Call your vet if your dog refuses to eat for more than one day or if the vomiting, diarrhea, or constipation do not stop within twenty-four hours.

Anesthetics have improved greatly over the last few years. Isoflurane gas anesthetic is one of the best, if not the best. Animals wake up from it faster than the other inhalants. Recovery is smooth with less hallucinating. And the safety factor is fantastic.

It is often convenient to do other procedures when Spike is under anesthesia. If Spike must undergo anesthesia, have as much done as possible. Have his teeth cleaned and polished, have any small lumps or warts removed, have his anal glands expressed, have his toenails trimmed, have his ears examined and cleaned if needed. If you are thinking of breeding Spike, have his hips X-rayed for hip dysplasia. While Spike is under anesthesia for the hip X-rays, if his hips are not good, have the vet neuter him right then so that you can avoid putting Spike under anesthesia again.

Vaccinations

Vaccination has become a very controversial subject in both human and animal medicine in recent years. As more and more vaccines become available, the risk of adverse reactions increases and the risk/benefit ratio of administering the vaccine comes into question. Many people believe that we may be overwhelming young developing immune systems with too many vaccines at once. The resultant damage may leave individuals more susceptible to health problems involving altered immune response such as allergies, asthma, and autoimmune diseases. An eight-week-old pup weighing two pounds receives the same vaccine and at the same dosage as an eight-week-old pup weighing fifteen pounds. Vaccines are formulated according to the species, not by the animal's weight.

When Spike receives a vaccination, he should be observed for a reaction. Small or toy breeds usually have a higher incidence of reactions. Reactions vary from difficulty breathing, vomiting, diarrhea, hives, pawing at the face, or shivering. This dog MUST be taken back to the veterinarian IMMEDIATELY! Some milder forms of reactions may not be noticeable for up to three weeks after a vaccination. Then, Spike may have a very mild seizure, or he may develop bumps on his skin. If Spike has some health changes within three weeks of receiving the vaccination, don't rule out a reaction to the injection just because it happened that long ago. Then again, it may not be related to the vaccination. Talk it over with your veterinarian and keep notes in case it happens the next time Spike receives a vaccination. If it does, the probability is high that it is related to the vaccine.

There are several things you can do to reduce the risk of reaction. Please consult with your veterinarian *beforehand* to be sure you are both comfortable with the way Spike will be taken care of.

Most distemper combination vaccines use leptospirosis as the liquid (or diluent) ingredient. The diluent is mixed with the distemper, adenovirus type 2, parainfluenza, and parvo (DA2PLP) powder to make an injectable vaccine. Portuguese water dog breeders use sterile water instead of leptospirosis as the diluent because their breed appears to have a reaction to the lepto vaccine if given during the first year of the dog's life. Lepto is omitted all through the puppy vaccinations. When Spike receives his first booster vaccine a year later, lepto is then used in the vaccine. Many breeders of other kinds of dogs have adopted this method to reduce the risk of reaction for their pups to leptospirosis; this virus seems to be triggering reactions in some dogs.

Another way to reduce the risk of vaccine reaction is to separate a few of the ingredients. Spike runs a higher risk of reaction when he is injected with a vaccine that contains seven viruses in one shot. If he was vaccinated with distemper, adenovirus type 2, and parainfluenza (DA2P) on one visit and vaccinated for parvo two weeks later, his risk of reaction would be lessened. Spike would then need to go to the veterinarian every two weeks for one vaccination or the other. More time consuming for you; safer for Spike. If this is not practical, consider giving Spike his rabies vaccination a few weeks before or after any other vaccinations.

Some breeds (e.g., rottweilers and Dobermans) seem much more susceptible to the parvo virus, for some unknown reason. (Studies are being done to see if their DNA is different from other breeds.) Giving them their last parvo vaccination after twenty weeks of age is recommended to ensure active immunity against this virus. It is important to be an informed owner and make choices appropriate for you and Spike. It has been proven that puppies that are not vaccinated are more susceptible to diseases and the possibility of dying from them.

Lyme disease vaccine rates among the more controversial vaccines. The initial Lyme disease vaccine was tested on fewer than fifty animals before a probational license was granted! From the beginning, it was suspect as to whether it actually protected Spike. It took over five years before another vaccine company was able to manufacture another Lyme vaccine. Studies at Cornell have concluded that over 90 percent of dogs exposed to Lyme disease develop natural immunity. If you live in an area where the disease is endemic, you might want to consider vaccinating. If not, you might want to think twice about whether Spike really needs the vaccine.

If you have a purebred dog (or a mixed breed but know the breeds involved in making up that litter), you can find out more information on specific health issues including whether that breed (or mixture) is more sensitive to certain vaccinations. There is a parent club for every recognized American Kennel Club, Canadian Kennel Club, or United Kennel Club breed. These organizations are listed in the back of this book and can provide you with a contact person in a specific breed organization. You can also get information on the Internet; most of the breed clubs have web pages.

Another alternative to giving Spike yearly vaccinations is to have a titre done. A titre will measure if Spike has enough antibodies to fight off an exposure to distemper or parvo. He might have enough antibodies to protect him from the viruses for a year or more (having titres done yearly is recommended). While the blood work may cost more than the yearly vaccinations, it is an option to consider for those of you who do not want Spike to have anything that is not completely necessary.

Heartworms, Ticks, Fleas, and Other Parasites

Heartworm is spread by mosquitoes that acquire larvae from dogs infected with adult heartworms. A heartworm preventative protects dogs by killing infective larvae before they can mature and form adults. Adults live in the right side chambers of the heart where they produce babies called microfilaria.

Are you living in an area that has heartworm? If so, check with your veterinarian to find out when Spike should have a blood sample tested to make sure he does not already have heartworm before putting him on the preventative. If Spike tests positive for heartworm and is accidentally put on daily preventative, he could become seriously ill or die from the reaction to the medication. Even in areas where heartworm preventative is given yearly to Spike, he should still have a yearly (some areas of the country are stretching that to every two years) blood test for heartworm to make sure the active ingredient in the preventative is working.

Heartworm preventative can be given on a daily or monthly basis. Daily heartworm medication comes in liquid or tablet form. This medication kills early stages of the microfilaria. If you miss giving the medication for a week (in some epidemic areas, even a few days), Spike could test positive the following year. The monthly heartworm preventative comes in chewables or tablets. This medication takes care of three stages of the microfilaria (larvae up to fifty to sixty days old). In other words, if a dog becomes infected through mosquitoes, this form of heartworm preventative once given will eliminate any larvae up to fifty to sixty days old.

Remember, the dosage for Spike is based on his weight. If you plan on using a daily form of preventative, make sure he is tested *before* giving any to him. Even if you did not miss a dose last year, he still needs to be checked this year to make sure he tests negative for heartworm. It may cost you a little more to do this, but the alternative is a dead dog.

Fleas and ticks are common in some areas of the country. In puppies, older dogs, or dogs in weakened conditions, these blood-sucking insects can do serious harm. There are many choices available to protect your animal from fleas and ticks. These choices include collars, tablets to be ingested, powders, and sprays or liquid to be placed on the animal's coat. Some of these products will last only until the dog gets wet; others will last a month or longer. Check with your veterinarian to find out what is right for you and Spike. Remember, if you pull a tick off Spike, there may be a lump in that area for up to a month.

Adulticide flea preventatives include Frontline, Advantage, and Defend; also available are flea collars, dips, powders, and sprays. These products kill adult fleas and/or deter them from living on Spike. Growth hormone regulator products are not an insecticide. Program is the most common one known. It prevents the eggs from hatching and renders the female flea sterile.

If you don't have a big problem with fleas and/or ticks but still want to cut down on what Spike brings into the house—and not use conventional methods—think about trying one of the following suggestions.

1. Cut up a lemon or orange into wedges (rind and all), put them into a gallon jug, and add $3/4$ of a gallon of water. Make sure the jug either has a solid cap to seal off the top or that it has a wide enough mouth that you can reach in with a big spoon. Either gently shake the jar periodically throughout the next few days or stir it briskly several times a day. After a few days, strain the mixture, keeping the water. With a plant mister, mist the solution onto your pet. You can do this daily, as it is not toxic to Spike.

2. Mist oil of pennyroyal directly onto Spike; use it sparingly and weekly.

3. Make your own flea collar out of cloth and scent it with oil of pennyroyal, citronella, cedar, or eucalyptus.

4. Mix garlic and brewer's yeast and give it to Spike at least a month **before** flea season starts. It takes a few

weeks to work through to the skin, where it acts as a flea repellent. (There are also commercial mixtures available in pet stores, pet supply catalogs, and human health food stores.)

During black fly season, black dogs, dogs with upright ears, puppies, and elderly dogs seem to be the fly's favorite targets. You can use human mosquito repellent sparingly on Spike. The roll-on type can be applied directly to his ears and under his eyes; put a stripe down his back and on his belly. Use the spray type sparingly. Spray some onto an old cloth and than wipe his face and ears; spray down his back and belly. You do not want him to try to lick either type off, so keep him busy and distracted for ten minutes or so after the application.

When mosquitoes bite Spike on his soft underbelly, you will notice a red ring about a half inch to an inch across. Sometimes there might be a bull's-eye center in the ring. Do not be alarmed; it will usually fade within a few days. This may look like a deer tick bite, but those are a little different.

A deer tick bite will have a red center, usually surrounded by several red rings of progressively larger sizes until the red just starts to streak outward—sometimes in one long streak and sometimes with several streaks radiating outward from the center dot. Most ticks do not latch onto an animal in the abdomen area; they like the ears, neck, and armpit areas best. When in doubt, have it checked out by your vet. Unfortunately, because of the amount of hair that Spike has, you will not usually see any redness.

If Spike develops Lyme disease, he will usually act lame in one leg. The lameness could then leave that leg and cause another leg to be sore and lame. He may become lethargic and not eat as well. Sometimes these symptoms take months to appear after a dog has been bitten by a deer tick. Check with your veterinarian; fast treatment is essential to prohibit lifelong problems.

Hookworms can kill a puppy; they attach themselves to the wall of the intestinal tract, suck blood, and cause life-threatening anemia. Some pups/dogs will need a life-saving blood transfusion.

Tapeworms are rarely identified under the microscope. These parasites usually pass segments that resemble small grains of rice. They can be found under Spike's tail or in his bedding. Tapeworms may cause Spike to rub his bottom on the floor. These parasites have indirect life cycles, meaning dogs acquire the parasite by ingesting another host such as a flea or rodent. Controlling fleas and ingestion of rodents will control tapeworms.

(Anal glands that need to be expressed may be another reason that Spike is rubbing his bottom along the floor. These are small sacs that are located on each side of his rectum. They are under the skin, where they fill up with secretions. Everytime Spike has a bowel movement, some of the liquid is expressed. Centuries ago this may have been a way for Spike to mark his territory. If enough fluid does not get expressed, it builds up pressure in the sac. If Spike is dragging his fanny on the floor, take him to the veterinarian and have the anal glands emptied.)

If Spike docs have parasites, you should be aware that medications sold over the counter in grocery stores, feed stores, or drugstores are less potent than the products a vet would use. Veterinary products are superior. If any reactions occur, your vet will know exactly what to do.

Use only the necessary medication. For example, if Spike has roundworms only, then using a medication that will take care of four other types of worms is not necessary and usually more expensive. Use only what is necessary; avoid overtreatment.

Take a fresh sample of his stool to the vet and have it tested. Fecal tests are designed to identify the presence of specific parasites by the presence of their eggs. But fecal tests have their limitations. If eggs are not being shed, you might get the false impression that Spike is free of parasites. If a parasite is suspected, most veterinarians will administer worm medication. This is especially practical with young puppies. Most puppies have parasites and should be wormed. Worming is usually repeated in three weeks. If you take Spike to areas where he meets a number of dogs or to areas that are favorite walking spots for dogs, his stool should be checked at least yearly for parasites (more frequently in warmer climates).

Parasites take on greater importance in warm climates, especially ones where summer temperatures exist six months or more. In colder climates, these parasites become dormant during the colder months.

Allergies

Allergies are caused by the reaction of allergens (proteins) with the immune system. Allergies are acquired. Food allergies may occur to foods that have been consumed for years. Just because Spike has always eaten brand x for years does not mean that he could not become allergic to his customary diet. Allergies to anything in the environment are possible. Simply put, if your pet scratches excessively, chews his feet, has chronic itchy waxy ears, or rubs his face excessively on things, maybe you should consider that Spike has allergic disease. Spike's diet may be all or part of the problem.

Here are a few other things to think about regarding allergic skin disease. Allergies that are seasonal (i.e., occur only at certain times of the year such as spring, summer, or fall) strongly suggest environmental influences rather than diet. Often a pattern can be established from year to year. For these dogs, short-term treatments such as glucocorticoids and fatty acid supplements are very satisfactory. Your veterinarian can help you with the different choices. Unfortunately, some dogs become allergic year round, in which case other treatments need to be sought out. For most of these patients, allergy testing and a desensitizing vaccination program will be necessary. These protocols are expensive, necessitate you learning to give injections, and may take three to six months before seeing any improvement. Treatment may often be lifelong. Success rates will vary but can be as high as 70 to 80 percent

There are two very important things to consider with *possible* allergic dogs. First, always rule out common causes of itching. These include fleas, skin infections, and sarcoptic mange (a mite). Before putting your dog through allergy testing and vaccine protocols, ask your vet to check for sarcoptic mange, which is often overlooked. This mange is 100 percent treatable and curable. Diagnosis is based on a positive skin scraping (seeing the mites under a microscope), but if the disease is suspected, it never hurts to treat it even if scrapings are negative.

Second, the body responds to allergens in a cumulative way (i.e., a slow buildup of grasses, food, pollens, and so on, produce a threshold reaction that culminates in symptoms). Trying a hypoallergenic diet even though Spike has a seasonal allergy may still prove helpful. Air filtering units that remove dust and pollens may help. Likewise, distilled water, frequent vacuuming, removing houseplants, covering furniture with plastic, and even removal of house rugs may prove effective.

Allergies can be very frustrating for Spike, you, and your vet. As an owner, you need to be patient in order to sort things out. Your vet may want to refer you to a veterinary dermatologist or allergist.

What if you or someone in your family develops allergies to Spike? Is it truly Spike that you are allergic to or the combination of him and other items such as dust mites, seasonal problems, and plants? One way to ensure that it is really Spike and not the combination is to place Spike with a friend or put him in a boarding kennel for three weeks. Totally clean the house, remove all scented candles, soaps, perfumes, and so on. Are you much improved without Spike or are you about the same? If you visit an allergist and he/she finds out that you have a pet, the first words of advice are usually to find the animal a new home. But sometimes it is not JUST the pet that has brought about these allergy problems.

Most people react to either the dandruff or saliva of the animal. The dandruff usually has some saliva on it from the animal cleaning himself. Washing your hands after touching Spike will help enormously. Washing your skin where Spike licks you will also reduce how strongly he affects your allergies. With a little more thought on your part, you can still keep Spike and deal with your allergies. It is your choice though. Using a spray or lotion on Spike to stop his shedding is not realistic. Most dogs shed—some year-round and some only twice a year; others, like the poodle, don't shed at all.

If you want a dog and you or someone in your family has allergies, try to spend time with the breed you want. How does the allergic person react to the dog and the environment? While poodles are the best-known breed for people with allergies, the following also cause less of a reaction than others:

- The Irish water spaniel was bred to hunt. He is the largest of the spaniels. As his name implies, he likes to swim. His hair coat (not fur) will continue to grow like a person's until it is cut. It is an active breed with a sense of humor that not everyone appreciates.
- The Portuguese water dog is a working dog. He is a little shorter than an Irish water spaniel. His coat also needs to be cut on a regular basis. A breed that is very active the first year or two and then calms down considerably.
- The Bichon Frise, Tibetan terrier, and some terriers are better for people who have allergies than other breeds.

Seizures

Seizures are expressions of erratic electrical discharges in the brain. There are two general classifications of epileptic seizures: petit mal and grand mal.

A petit mal seizure is usually missed unless you are looking for it. The dog may start walking across the room, stop for a few seconds gazing off into space, and than continue on. He may act as if he is watching a bug on a wall. Or he may be playing, stop and act as if he is in another world, and then resume playing.

A grand mal seizure is one where the dog falls to the floor, foams at the mouth, twitches his skin, moves his legs as if he were running in place, and loses control of his body functions. He is not really aware of where he is or what is going on. Simply put, he blacks out. This usually only lasts three to five minutes.

There are many causes for seizures. Your vet will perform exams and order tests to help define their cause. However, despite those tests, the cause is not always identified. Epileptic medication is indicated to *control* seizures. Rarely are seizures ever cured. (In some rare cases, changing dog food has stopped some dogs from having any more seizures.)

Depending on how often the dog has a seizure, he may or may not need daily medication. Keep a diary and record what time of day the dog had a seizure. Did you have company within seventy-two hours of the seizure? Did a family member leave for college? Did you get a new carpet? Did you have a fumigator in to take care of pests? Did a neighbor have their lawn chemically treated? Are you washing his bedding in a new detergent? Record anything out of the ordinary; it could be a clue to what set off the dog.

Not all seizures are epileptic. Seizures can occur if the dog has low blood sugar; has been exposed to lead, insecticides, rodent poisoning, certain plants, or carbon monoxide; has parasites; has ingested part of a poisonous plant; or has had a head injury.

When a dog has a seizure, it can be very scary to watch. Usually by the time you phone the vet, the dog is coming out of the seizure. During a seizure, Spike may lose control of his bladder and bowels. He will NOT swallow his tongue, so do not try to grab it. Keep him away from stairs, objects with sharp edges such as coffee tables and fireplace hearths, bodies of water, and so on. During the recovery phase at the end of a seizure, Spike will be wobbly and not very coordinated when he tries to walk. He should be kept quiet and in one spot until he is able to walk normally.

Urinary Tract Infections

Whether Spike is male or female, if he/she seems to have one urinary tract infection after another, you may want to do a little detective work. If you live in an older house that has copper pipes or if you have a well, Spike may be receiving too many minerals in his drinking water. Give Spike distilled water for a month or so and see if that improves his bladder infection. Putting him on a low-protein (less than 20 percent) diet may also help. Also, try cranberry tablets. Cranberry will change the pH of the urine and reduce the bacteria in the bladder. Always take a urine sample to the veterinarian first to see if Spike has a bladder infection. If he does not have an infection but wants to go out to the bathroom more frequently than you think is necessary, try the above suggestions.

Cold or Dead Tail

This usually occurs when Spike has been given a bath with cold water, when he has been allowed to air dry during a cool day, or when someone has given a tug on his tail. The tail will be normal from the base and down a few inches. Then the tail hangs almost lifelessly. He may not want to wag it. He may also act uncomfortable.

This will usually go away on its own within a few days. Giving Spike an aspirin (check with vet for dosage) twice a day may speed up the recovery.

Medications and How to Give Them

When giving prescribed medications to Spike, give them as the label indicates. If the label says to give the medication twice a day for ten days that means every twelve hours for ten days. It does not mean that you give the medication at 8 A.M. and again at 1 P.M. and consider that medication being given twice a day.

Don't stop the medication because Spike seems to have recovered. You need to give the medication for the duration indicated or Spike could have a relapse. Next time, it may take longer for him to get better.

Only give human medication to Spike upon advice from your veterinarian! Some human medications, while similar to dog medications, do not react the same way with animals. What helps you may kill your dog.

Aspirin may be given to Spike if he is sore. Coated aspirin is preferred. If Spike cannot tolerate coated aspirin, he probably will not be able to keep down non-steriodial anti-inflammatory medications (e.g., Motrin, Advil, and Aleve) that are used for arthritic conditions, bad backs, or pulled muscles.

How do you give Spike a tablet or capsule of medicine? Most dogs will take it readily if it is coated with something like butter or peanut butter. Hiding it in a piece of cheese (cheese logs are great for this—the nuts camouflage the pill) or meat will work even better. If you only give Spike one piece of food with the tablet/capsule in it, he will probably resist taking it after a few days. Try having two to three pieces of food handy, one of which has the medication in it. Sometimes feed Spike the piece with the medication in it first, sometimes second, and sometimes third. Hold those treats right in front of his nose so that he is in a hurry to finish one in order to get the next one.

Some dogs need to have the medication literally shoved down their throats. If you are right handed, put the medication between your thumb and first finger. Either straddle Spike or get him up against a piece of furniture, a wall, or the kitchen cupboards so that you can hold him in place. With your left hand, gently take hold of his muzzle and lift his head toward the ceiling. With the rest of the fingers of your right hand, open up his mouth, insert the medication as far back as you can get it, and close his mouth. Keep his head pointing at the ceiling until he has swallowed. If you allow him to lower his head before he swallows, he will most likely spit out the pill. With small dogs, wrapping a large bath towel around them and putting them on a piece of furniture may be easier for you. Or wrapping Spike up in the towel and putting him between your knees as you kneel on the floor will work too.

Giving Spike liquid medication may be more of a challenge. You usually end up with more on you than you are able to get into Spike. Again, you may need to restrain him in some fashion. Have the liquid ready in one hand while you gently pull out his lower lip by his back teeth with the other hand. This will make a pocket to put the liquid in. As soon as you do, tilt his head back to encourage him to swallow the medication. Rubbing his throat will usually bring on a swallow or two. If you open up his mouth and try to pour the liquid in, he may inhale the medicine, which could cause inhalation pneumonia.

To put ointment in his eyes, you'll need to tip his head back slightly. While one hand holds the eyelids apart, the other hand squeezes the medication into the lower eyelid. Aiming for the lower eyelid will keep the nozzle of the tube of ointment away from Spike's eyeball, reducing the chance of the nozzle scraping on the eye itself. It takes very little of the ointment to do the job; don't put in so much that it runs over the eyelid and out. Giving Spike a yummy treat afterward may help him to accept treatment.

With some dogs, giving any type of medication may be a two-person job. Each time, no matter how much Spike struggles, try to get him to relax before letting him go; then give him extra attention and a treat or toy.

Hyperactivity and/or Anxiety

Certain foods or combinations of food, preservative, and color additives can make some dogs hyper. If Spike is still wound up after a thirty to sixty-minute run, during which he can go at his own pace, you may want to consider changing his food. If changing the food does not seem to work, you can try human StressTabs with Zinc. This vitamin B complex helps in calming hyper/anxious people. Since it is a water soluble vitamin, what Spike does not use is flushed out of his body. You may notice his urine is a slightly different color. For the average size dog, fifty pounds and up, one a day is sufficient.

Prozac is being used with success on animals with compulsive disorders such as constant tail chasing, flank sucking, or self-mutilation. This medication is expensive. You may want to consult an animal behaviorist to see if Spike's problem is behavioral and can be corrected without having to resort to medications.

Human antianxiety/anti-depressant medications are being used on dogs with high degrees of stress or anxiety. These medications are usually very successful in calming Spike and helping him be a little more mellow without making him act sleepy (antianxiety medication is NOT like a tranquilizer). Before consulting with your vet about medications like these, be honest with yourself about how much exercise Spike really gets. You may think it is enough, but Spike may not think so!

For those of you who would rather find alternative methods to so-called drugs, herbs such as St. John's Wort and Kava Kava have a beneficial effect on anxious people and animals. Dogs over fifty pounds should receive an adult person's dose. Dogs under fifty pounds should receive half of that dose.

Some dogs may be hyper or appear stressed due to having a low thyroid count. Some dogs are the opposite; they gain weight easily, have a dry, dull coat, and are lethargic. Both types of dogs may benefit from having blood taken and sent off to have their thyroid levels checked. If too low, there is medication available. With dogs, the generic form, Soloxine, works better than the human form, Synthroid, and is less expensive. Dogs on thyroid medication will still need to be periodically checked to make sure adjustments are not needed with their medication.

Mood swings, bizarre behavior, separation anxiety, and/or a Jekyll and Hyde personality are all symptomatic of a low thyroid count and call for a thyroid screening. Medication resolves most of these issues.

Sometimes Spike will pick up on the tension or emotions in the home and become hyper or anxious. If that is the case, the medications may not help. Dogs feel our emotions and respond to them. Stop for a minute and really think about what may be causing Spike to behave this way. If you can find a way to reduce the stress you are under, you probably won't need to put Spike on any medication.

There's a new drug called Clomicalm to help dogs who have separation anxiety. Only one out of every four dogs labeled as such really has this problem. With the others, the issue is mostly lack of leadership, training, and management, which no amount of medication will make up for. With any medication, you want to retrain the dog and than wean him off of it. Spike should not be on medication for life except in rare instances. For those dogs with true separation anxiety, this medication along with training can make a huge difference and actually be in some cases a life-saver. Along with the above medications and herbs, a retraining program put together by a behaviorist is necessary to achieve full benefit and have Spike be a better dog.

Vomiting and Diarrhea

There are many reasons why Spike has this problem. Maybe the ingredients in the bag of food have been changed or are moldy. Maybe he ate something out in the yard, got into some garbage, or drank stagnant water. Whatever the reason, what can you do about it?

First, if Spike is acting his normal self, seems bright, alert, eyes bright and clear, he can go without food and water for twenty-four hours. This gives the stomach and intestinal tract a chance to calm down and pass whatever is the problem, be it an object or bacterial.

Than for the next two to three days, Spike needs to eat a bland diet of either boiled hamburger meat or boneless, skinless chicken meat. Cook up a batch of white rice (not Minute rice, which is not effective) and feed the meat and rice to Spike. He should start to have formed stools within a day.

If he is still vomiting or having diarrhea, he needs to see a veterinarian without any more delay! There could be a foreign body stuck someplace within the stomach or intestinal tract that might need surgery to remove it only his doctor can know for sure.

If Spike is not his normal self, if his eyes are weepy or have a discharge, if he acts lethargic, or if he seems sore to the touch anyplace, he needs to be checked out thoroughly by the veterinarian immediately. Be sure to take along a stool sample. The vet will want to eliminate the possibility that parasites are the cause of the diarrhea.

Choosing a Veterinarian

Choosing a veterinarian is like finding the right doctor for yourself. Can you talk to him/her? Are you given enough time to go over your concerns? Are you comfortable with the answers to your questions? Does the vet handle his/her own emergencies after regular office hours or does he/she refer clients to an emergency clinic in the area?

Talk to your friends; see who they go to with their pets. Call the veterinarian's office and ask the receptionist for an appointment to meet with the vet and see how you like the place, the staff, and the vet. Are they friendly and helpful? Can you get a tour of the hospital/clinic? Do things look clean, organized, up to date, in good shape? Is there an overall odor that seems to have seeped into the walls, or is there a clean smell?

If you have not been to a veterinarian in a while and have a new puppy, call around and ask the receptionists what happens when you bring a puppy to the vet for the first visit. If the receptionist says, "The vet checks the pup over, gives him a vaccination if needed at that time, weighs him, and sends you to me to pay your bill," go somewhere else. This type of vet is not trying to make the pup's first visit a positive experience.

This is what you want to hear: "We love puppies! The vet or the tech will go over house-training, puppy classes, nutrition, and crate training. We will spend about a half hour with you and your pup. The pup will be put on the examining table, given treats, put on the floor, and have this done several times both before and after the vet examines the pup. We want him to feel good about coming here and being with us."

Some vets have good bedside manners; others do not. Some people want the vet to make the decisions; others want to be informed so that they can make their own decision. Whichever type of vet you choose, it is up to you to make sure you understand the reason the vet is doing the procedure to Spike, whether it involves blood tests, X-rays, or surgery. Ultimately it is up to you to be responsible for making decisions and paying the bill. The name of the game is COMMUNICATION!

When you have a good working relationship with your vet and his/her staff, you will find that they will go out of their way to help you and your pet. They might give a little extra attention to Spike before surgery, a little pampering out of a cage while recovering, an extra treat when allowed, or extra walks to help Spike be less stressed.

Sometimes a pup or dog becomes frightened of going to the vet. To ensure that the dog does not become more frightened, he needs to understand that every trip to the vet is not going to result in an injection or a stay there. To accomplish this, call ahead and find out when the animal hospital is less busy. Make sure it is okay to go over for a short visit. Take along Spike's favorite treats, and if anyone is available to help, let them feed a few treats to Spike. Keep the visit short and fun if you can. If he is not that keen on treats and would rather have a toy instead, take his favorite toy along. Interact with him and the toy. See if any of the workers there can come out and play for a few minutes too. If you do this a few times a week for several weeks, Spike will loose some of his fear of the vet's office. Once he is doing better, see if you can put him up on an exam table, as this is a source of fear for most dogs. Continue to do the visits until he feels more comfortable at the vet's office. If at any time he becomes fearful again, just start making the visits again.

Euthanasia

Unless Spike passes away from natural causes (and most dogs do not), you will at some time be faced with the uncomfortable decision of whether to put Spike to sleep or let him go on living. It is always hard to think about the loss of a loved one; it is even harder to be the individual making the decision as to when his life will end. You need to be fair with yourself and Spike. Is he suffering? Has his quality of life deteriorated to the point that he has lost his dignity? You do not want to remember him clinging on with no dignity, poor health, pain, and suffering. The animal world is fortunate to have veterinarians who are there to help these animals and their owners. Upon request, they can humanely put an animal to sleep with a simple intravenous injection. You can stay with Spike while this is performed if you so choose.

Some owners request a simple cremation of the remains. If you inquire, ashes can be returned, but this decision needs to be made before Spike is cremated. If desired, you could bury the remains in your yard, providing local ordinances do not forbid it.

Having a plan for Spike's last living moments and care of his remains ahead of time will make the moment a little easier for you when the time comes. If you know how you want Spike taken care of after he has been put to sleep, inform your veterinarian. If your request is already written in Spike's record, you will be a little less stressed when that day comes. Try to remember the pet for the good times—the joy, fun, and companionship he provided.

It sometimes helps to have a family member or friend with you when you make this last decision for Spike. Some people make the appointment with the vet and then spend the rest of the day with Spike, taking him to all of his favorite places and letting him eat his favorite foods. You need to do what feels right for you.

Once Spike is gone, you will find some support from friends. However, unless those friends also have animals, they may not truly understand the degree of grief you are feeling. They will try to be supportive but may eventually say that you need to get on with life. If you feel you need to talk to someone who will truly understand your depth of feeling for Spike, find other dog people, either at a dog class or dog shows, or consult a dog behaviorist. People who have experienced the loss of a loved pet will not push you to end your grieving process before you are ready to. There are support groups available to help anyone deal with the loss of a pet. Contact your local hospital to find the nearest hospice group. Someone in the group will either be aware of how to help grieving pet owners or know of someone who can.

Some people plant a tree or bush in memory of Spike. Others donate to a humane shelter or to organizations that try to improve the lives of animals through better food, health, or education. Still others have a rock engraved with Spike's name and the years he spent on earth. Again, do whatever feels right for you.

First Aid

The normal heart rate is between 80 and 120 beats per minute, depending on the age and size of the dog. Smaller dogs have faster heart rates than larger dogs. Giant breeds have slower rates than larger dogs. Practice checking his heart rate when Spike is lying down and resting. Place your hand between the floor and his chest, close to his arm pit area. Lightly rest your fingers and hand on his rib cage and slowly move your hand until you can feel his heart beating. Count the beats for fifteen seconds and multiply by four or count for a full minute.

A dog's normal rectal temperature is usually between 100.4 and 102.5 degrees. If the dog has exercised, it is hot outside, or he is not feeling well, his temperature will be elevated. When his temperature is over 104 degrees, you should call the veterinarian.

Dogs are unable to regulate body temperature as well as we do. It is important that you do not play strenuous games during the hottest part of the day; dogs can easily become overheated. If he wants to play fetch, find a stream, river, or lake for him to retrieve in. A child's wading pool is a great way to help keep him cool! A dog needs shade in the warm weather as well as in the cold. If you want Spike to spend a fair amount of time outside during the colder months, gradually let him stay out for longer and longer periods of time starting in the early fall. In this manner, he will become conditioned to the changing temperatures.

The following caveats bear repeating: Chocolate can be deadly for Spike! It contains theobromine and caffeine, which can cause problems. Baking chocolate contains about nine times more theobromine than milk chocolate. Onions are also toxic to Spike, either cooked or raw. Signs of chocolate or onion toxicity are vomiting, hyperactivity, increased heart rate, and diarrhea. Call your veterinarian immediately if you suspect that Spike has eaten candy or onions.

If Spike has swallowed something potentially dangerous or poisonous, call your veterinarian IMMEDIATELY! If he/she recommends that you induce vomiting before bringing Spike into the hospital, here are three agents you can use to make him vomit:

1. A heavy salt (called a brine) solution in water can be administered slowly between his lips on the side of his

mouth. If you pour it too rapidly into Spike, there is a chance the liquid could go into his lungs instead of his stomach and cause inhalation pneumonia.

2. Hydrogen peroxide may be administered the same way.

3. Ipecac syrup is a very potent emetic (vomiting agent) that requires much less volume. It is usually kept around exclusively for children, but it also works well on dogs.

Large breeds, giant breeds, and dogs with deep chests are more susceptible to gastric torsion, but any dog can have one. A torsion occurs when the stomach rotates 180 to 360 degrees and shuts off the dog's ability to vomit or pass food out of his stomach. The dog starts to bloat, looking like he swallowed a basketball. This needs IMMEDIATE attention!

It is felt that a contributing cause to this condition is feeding Spike and letting him play hard right afterward. Feeding him while he is still panting from exercise is not wise either. Wait at least an hour after exercise before feeding Spike. Have Spike wait at least several hours after eating before allowing him to exercise.

If your dog is hurt in an accident, you might want to muzzle him before trying to move him. Any dog will bite if he is in enough pain. You can make a muzzle out of rope, a piece of sheet, or a leg from pantyhose. Do not be concerned about having it loose enough for the dog to breath; he can do that just fine through his nose. But if it is too loose, he could bite you or give you a very bad pinch. The muzzle will stay on best if you wrap it several times around his nose and mouth, tie it once under his jaw tightly, and then take the ends up behind his ears and tie it off snugly. Now if he hooks his front feet over the part on his nose, he will not be able to pull it off.

Check for signs of shock by first checking your dog's gums. Press firmly into a pink section of his gums with your thumb or finger. When you remove your thumb or finger, the color should return promptly, within one to two seconds. Look at your dog's gums regularly so that you can identify what is normal. If he is in shock but is able to walk, he should still be taken to the vet's immediately; he may have internal bleeding.

If Spike has been injured so that he can't walk, use a blanket or board as a stretcher to lift him; you want to keep his back straight to avoid further injury to a broken bone or spine. To put Spike on a board or blanket, put it on the ground against Spike's back. Try to keep the back in the same position as it looks to you with him on the ground. If you lift one end of Spike to put it on the board or blanket and he has a fractured back, you could make it much worse. Keeping that in mind, get behind Spike and try to pull him onto the board or blanket by putting one hand on the scruff of his neck and the other on his rump. Gently pull Spike toward you. If you have someone to help you, make sure you both pull him at the same time to keep the back in the same alignment.

If Spike is small enough that you can pick him up, do so by placing one hand across the front of his chest and the other under his abdomen. This will help to keep his back straighter. If you pick him up with one hand across his chest and the other just below his tail across the back of his hips, you will arch his back when you pick him up. If he has a back injury, it will thus be made worse.

When you put Spike into the car, try to keep him as still as possible. You may need to call a friend or neighbor over to help you get him into the car and sit with him on the ride to the vet.

If you need to transport your dog to the veterinary hospital, have someone call ahead to notify the veterinarian that you are on your way, but DO NOT leave until you know the vet is going to be there. Do this even during the vet's normal working hours. What if he was called away from the office? If he is closed and you need to go to another vet or emergency clinic, do you know where to go? Trying to find a new place when you are stressed is very nerve-racking and may cause loss of valuable time.

Any bleeding should be controlled by applying direct pressure to the wound. If possible, apply a pressure bandage before taking him to the vet. Either use a bunch of paper towels, a clean towel folded up, or sanitary pads to help stop the flow of blood. This will help to control the loss of blood (and help to keep your car cleaner). Do not use a tourniquet.

Cut foot pads can bleed profusely. Clean and inspect the wound. Then apply a clean, dry bandage. Have the vet check the foot to make sure there is not something in there (e.g., a piece of glass or metal) that will cause the wound to fester.

Be careful to keep the bandage dry at all times. If Spike goes outside when the ground is wet, the bandage will get wet, and the wound will take longer to heal and may even get infected. Put a plastic bag over the bandage and either tape it to the bandage or Spike's leg or put an elastic around it to help hold it on. Be sure to take off the plastic bag and especially the elastic when Spike comes back in the house. Keeping the plastic bag on will create moisture within the bandage, creating the very problem you are trying to prevent. Letting the elastic band stay on the leg may be snug enough to slow down the circulation in that leg. And never bandage a wound with waterproof tape. If the wound cannot "breathe," it will retain moisture and become infected.

A puncture wound or small cut may not seem like a big deal, but most such wounds make larger tears under the skin and need to be seen as soon as possible by a veterinarian. To leave such a wound invites bacteria to form and make an abscess. Then Spike will really need to see the vet.

Any bump or lump that suddenly starts to ooze should be seen by a vet. While it probably is not an emergency, Spike should be seen within a couple days.

Again, make sure you know whether your veterinarian does his/her own emergencies after regular office hours, refers clients to another vet at another location, or refers clients to an emergency clinic nearby. It is very stressful to have an emergency and not be sure where you are taking Spike for help. Keep the phone numbers listed where everyone can find them. If you are by yourself and send a friend into the house to make the phone call for help, can that person easily find the number? Do you know how to get to the other animal hospitals or emergency clinics?

You might also ask your veterinarian what to include in your own first-aid kit for Spike. It is helpful to have one around the house and especially when traveling.

Chapter 21

Multiple Dogs

Having more than one dog in the house can be fun, and it means your pet now has a friend (usually). Some breeds do not get along well with each other or other breeds, and sometimes having two of the same sex is not a great idea. Usually, it is a safe bet to have a male dog and a female dog for companions. Sometimes two males can be great together, depending on the breeds involved, ages, and who is most dominant. But two male dogs that fight will cause damage, though the fights will not usually prove fatal. Some females can be okay together; others will fight. Two female dogs can fight to the death of one or both of them.

A silent fight or altercation usually ends with a person or dog getting bitten. In this situation, the dog does not growl or warn of his intentions, except for staring at the dog or person. If you are observant, you may notice the stare before he lunges toward you or another dog. Usually firmly telling him to back off will stop the attack, but not always. Yelling sometimes makes matters worse. And don't wave your arms around, as that action will probably provoke an attack. Standing still and talking firmly is best. You draw attention from the dog to you in an abrupt manner which puts the dog on alert. Being strange or frightening (to the dog) usually results in a bite.

The more noise the dogs make, *usually* the less damage there is. Try to differentiate between talking and growling in each of your dogs so that you know when they are going to fight.

When you are bringing home another dog, it is best that they meet in a neutral area, not the house or yard. Have a few shake cans or something that will make a loud noise in case you need to distract the dogs from each other. Have someone hold one dog on a leash while you hold the other. Verbally reward appropriate behavior. Avoid using food as a reward until the dogs know each other better; otherwise, it may become an issue with one of the dogs. Ignore or correct the unwanted behavior as much as possible. Walk by each other with over forty feet between the two dogs. Walk back and forth and gradually get closer, BUT not close enough for them to sniff each other. Both of you sit down about ten feet apart with the dogs being the furthest apart. Talk to each other and observe the dogs. If there is no growling, after a few minutes, take the leashes off and tell them to "Go Play." It is best to do this in a fenced in area so that you can let go of the leashes. Ignore the dogs. If they know you are nervous, they will react more strongly against each other.

At any time that you feel the need to step in and correct one of the dogs, you must correct BOTH dogs! It is like having two children who are playing. One (Mike) teases the other (Adam) until that child retaliates. Now Adam gets into trouble. Mike has learned to tease and get Adam into trouble, so he will continue to do so unless he is punished also. The same is true with dogs. Rover may have eyed Spike and thus started the argument, but if Spike goes for Rover, he is the one who gets penalized.

When walking multiple dogs, have a separate leash for each dog. If you couple them together and a stray dog comes along and starts a fight, you will have all the dogs in the fight and not be able to get close enough to release any of them. If one dog feels the other dog is causing his collar to be tightened and correcting him when he does not need the correction, they can also turn on each other and fight.

When handing out treats, toys, pats, cuddle time, and so on, do so first with the dominant dog. If you give first to the underdog, you will cause the dominant dog to pick on him more for not respecting the pecking order. The underdog does, of course, understand the pecking order, so you will not be hurting his feelings by giving first to the dominant dog. If you don't know yet who will be the dominant dog, to avoid problems, hand the treats, toys, and pats out at the same time.

To know who is the dominant dog, watch to see who is out the door first when you let them go out. Who is the first to come to you for attention? (Sometimes a younger dog will be first in these two instances, but he may not be the dominant dog, just quicker!) If one dog is first but the other dog can push him away, the second dog is the dominant one. Who can make the other one look away when they are both looking at the same toy? Who can take a toy away from the other one? (Sometimes the dominant one will allow a younger dog to take a toy from him.) Who mounts the other one regardless of the sex of the dogs? The leader may change from room to room. The primary areas are (1) the main meeting area of the family, (2) the area where the dogs get fed, (3) the bedroom, (4) the yard, and (5) the car. They don't call the dominant dog the "Top Dog" for nothing. With observation, you will be able to find a pattern to see which of the dogs is truly in charge.

With multiple dogs, it is best to feed them in separate areas, preferably in crates or at least in separate rooms. If Rover is able to leave his food bowl, go and push Spike away from his bowl and eat it all, and still eat his own food, he is too dominant and will soon try to take you on! Having one dog go from bowl to bowl causes stress to the other dogs and eventually will result in a fight.

Dogs will work out who the dominant one is. Stay out of any ruckuses that might ensue during the learning process! The more you interfere, the more the dogs will argue and fight. Your feelings may be more hurt than the dog's if the first dog is not the top dog. If the new dog is the true top dog and you can't adjust, you should reconsider having two dogs at this time. Sometimes the dogs will only fight if you come into the room in an effort to get your attention—because you probably yelled and raced toward them in the past when they started in on each other. Turn your back and walk away. Do they stop on their own within ten to twenty seconds? If so, it is you that sets off the altercation. You need to have the dogs separate until you work this out. If they do not stop when you leave the room, you will need to go back and separate them.

Changing how the dogs view each other and you will be a big step in halting any problems. You may have been giving more attention to the first dog when the new dog was out of the room. Just like bringing home a baby, if you give attention to the dog when the baby is out of the room, the dog wants the child removed faster and more often each day to receive more and more attention from you. Do the opposite. Only give the first dog attention when the new dog is around. If you have a pup as the second dog and he takes a nap, ignore the older dog. When someone is home to watch the pup, that is the time to take the older dog for a walk or give him some attention. If you live by yourself, take the first dog for a walk once in a while when the pup has a nap. You want them to like doing things together, so reserve walks and other physical activities for when they both can do them. Try not to give a lot of patting or spend a lot of time with the first dog when the puppy is napping. Pups grow up fast, and he won't always need a nap. Your first dog will not understand this and want more and more attention.

If you have a pup as the second dog, most older dogs will tolerate a pup's antics for just so long before they have had enough. The older dog will growl at the pup. If the pup does not back off, he will raise his lips and show his teeth. If that does not slow down the pup, he will either pin the puppy (if he feels the need to get the message across) or just turn and walk away. If you interfere during these important lessons, you will make it more difficult for the older dog to correct the pup when he feels the need to do so. Most older dogs will put up with a lot from a pup until the pup's adult teeth come in. Then the older dog will usually start setting up guidelines for the pup. This lets the pup know when he is being too pushy, when the older dog wants to be left alone, when the older dog thinks the younger one is out of line, and so on. This is normal dog behavior; you should not relate it to human behavior. As the pup gets a little older you may hear both dogs growling. Or perhaps they are just talking to each other. Separate the two of them. Does the pup try to go back and play with the older dog? If so, let them play some more. If the pup stays with you when you separate the two of them, the pup may not be ready for the rougher play or it may be time for a nap.

Do both dogs view you as the leader? Are you eating first before they do? Are they both sleeping on the floor or in crates? You should not allow one dog on the bed and make the other sleep in a crate. Both dogs know and object to this by acting out. Are you fair and equal with the time you spend with each of them? Do you give more treats or pats to one than the other? This will also cause friction between the dogs. Dogs normally have very good social skills with each other and do quite well *IF* you do not interfere unless you absolutely have to.

If you have two dogs and get a third, or take the two to play with other dogs, you need to watch for what is called a tag-team. The two dogs will take turns chasing another dog, usually to the point of scaring it. Whenever you observe this, you should stop it. This behavior could escalate to a fight with both dogs ganging up on the other one.

Chapter 22

Bringing Home Baby

Once you know you are pregnant, it's time to start training Spike to accept a baby. Get a small doll and dress it every day. Sleep with the doll's clothes so that they smell of you. Start to wear a little perfume and put some on the doll and/or its clothes. It will help Spike make the adjustment from doll to baby easier. Pick the doll up as soon as you walk into the house. Spike gets greeted second. When you leave, say goodbye to Spike and then the doll. Spike is now being relegated to a lower ranking order in the family "pack."

Make sure that Spike is fed when the doll is out and being held. Most interactions with Spike are done when the doll is visible. When the doll has gone for a nap, interact less with Spike.

Once the baby comes home, don't ignore Spike. If possible, dress the baby in the doll's clothes. Dabbing just the smallest amount of your perfume onto the baby's clothes will also help

Spike realize that this little bundle is related to you. Putting a little perfume on the baby a couple of times a week will help Spike remember this. It will also be a big help when the baby starts to crawl. Spike will relate this little funny (to him) creature on the floor trying to move with the one you have been holding in your arms these past few months.

You want Spike to enjoy seeing the doll rather than resent it. The same is true when the baby comes home. If you put Spike away every time the baby comes out, he will not like the baby. If Spike has attention, play time, massage time, tricks taught, and so on, while the baby is out, he will look forward to having the baby around. When the baby is not around, do not do much with Spike.

Whenever the baby is placed on the floor, have Spike lie down nearby but out of reach of the baby; you don't want Spike suddenly being grabbed by the baby—it would ruin the start of a good relationship. Teach him what are his toys and what are the baby's. One of the easiest ways to do this is to spray Spike's toy with a different scent than the baby's. For example, Spike's toys could smell of cinnamon and the baby's of your perfume. Dogs have a great sense of smell, so it won't take much at all to leave a scent on the toys. If Spike has any favorite toys, make sure they are not out on the floor when the baby starts to crawl. If the baby crawled in the direction of the toy, Spike might become protective of it.

Supervision is the word when dealing with children, regardless of age, and a dog! If you leave baby on the floor when you leave to answer the phone in another room, encourage Spike to follow you. Even breeds of dogs who are typically great with children have exceptions. All it takes for Spike to snap is for a child to reach and grab the dog's tail, skin, or ear and give a quick tug.

Puppies understand that a dog's growl means "Leave me alone"; children do not speak dog language. So they are more apt to be bitten when no adult is around to make sure Spike is not being pushed past his limits.

There are several good books on dealing with children and dogs (see the book list at the back of this book). Above all, use common sense, and you should do just fine.

Introducing a Child

Spike should be introduced to children properly, one at a time. If you allow children to overwhelm a pup or a dog, you set Spike up to feel uncomfortable and possibly afraid of children.

Before allowing Spike to take a treat from ANYONE, make sure he takes the treat GENTLY. Also make sure that he does not have any ear problems. Most people, children and adults, like to scratch a dog around his ears. If his ears are sore or infected, Spike will not have a good experience, and it may possibly teach him to not like people reaching toward him.

Get Spike's favorite toy and sit with the child on one side of you and Spike on the other. Once he understands that you approve of the child, he will go along with the program more quickly and easily.

Have the child put his hand out palm up and flat, with a treat in the center of his/her hand. Tell Spike that the child is a "friend" and let Spike go up and get the treat.

Once Spike is okay with this, allow the child to reach under Spike's chin and give him a scratch. You need to be relaxed but alert. If you are tense, Spike will think you are upset with the child. This in turn will cause Spike to dislike or even growl at the child.

Bring a toy out and hand it to the child. Have the child toss it just in front of Spike and let Spike get it. Take the toy away from Spike and hand it back to the child. Have the child throw it a little further away from Spike. In a short period of time, Spike will be retrieving the toy and bringing it back to the child. If Spike does not retrieve the toy, he is still learning that the child means no harm.

If Spike mounts and starts to hump a child's leg, pull Spike off and give him a time-out. If the child laughs at Spike, the dog may try it again, thinking the child enjoyed the action. Even if the child did not laugh, Spike may try it again; he may be trying to dominate the child. The dominance issue can be dealt with by having the child feed Spike his meal and only putting the dish down if Spike minds the child on the first command to either "Sit" or "Down."

Chapter 23

Introducing a Cat

Introducing Spike to a cat is much like introducing him to a baby. Have the cat out in the same room with Spike for short periods of time (with some dogs, thirty seconds is enough) while the dog gets some quiet attention.

Gradually increase the time the cat is out with the dog. The cat should NEVER be out with the dog unsupervised if there is a reason for concern. If Spike starts to stare and look like he is about to stalk the cat, remove Spike as fast as possible. If you remove the cat, Spike will have learned how to get you to move the cat into another room. He should be the one to leave the room if he cannot behave himself.

Only feed Spike his meals when the cat is not around. You will not know if Spike will be protective of his food until he has the cat by the neck and is trying to kill it. Try feeding him a treat in another room with the cat around so that you can gauge his reaction to the cat and food being in the same room. While he may be okay with the cat and receiving a treat in that room, he may not do so well when the cat is in the room he normally eats his meals in. That would be the next step. Take the cat into the room where Spike usually eats his meals. Have the cat walk around and have Spike on a leash so that you have control of him and will be able to stop him from reaching the cat. Give Spike a treat and watch how he reacts with the cat being there. If he goes for the cat, remove Spike from the room; from then on the cat should not be in that room when it is time to feed the dog.

If the dog is chasing the cat and the cat has claws and is willing to confront Spike, let it happen. The more you interfere, the more Spike will chase the cat as a way for you to pay attention to him.

If the cat is old, declawed, or sick, Spike should not be allowed to give chase. Teach him the command "Leave It." Once he responds well to *leave it* for other objects of attraction, use it in regard to the cat.

With time, patience, and understanding about how the two species view each other, you should be able to have both a dog and a cat live together and accept each other. However, there is always the exception to the rule. You may have to decide to give up one of the animals or keep them in separate parts of the house, never to meet.

Cat food is higher in protein and fat, which makes it a delicacy to dogs. They will eat it before Kitty can, so put the food someplace where the cat can get it but Spike cannot. Due to the flavor, calories, and ingredients, Spike also likes to eat the cat poop. To avoid this habit, keep the litter box in an area that the cat can get to but the dog cannot. Some litter boxes have covers. However, while keeping Spike out, they are not as ventilated as most cats would like them to be. If you clean the litter box on a daily basis, this type of box may be used. Otherwise, the cat may decide the box is too stinky and use the floor.

Chapter 24

Choosing a Kennel, Sitter, Dog Walker, or Day Care

You need a break from Spike even if it is just overnight. Spike will do better and be less stressed if you do this before he is a year old. A lot of people never go away even for an overnight for a whole year once they get a puppy. Can you imagine the stress this dog goes through when the owner finally takes a vacation and goes away for two weeks?

If you want to board Spike, go look at the boarding kennels in your area. Don't call ahead; just show up and ask for a tour. Is it clean? Is there an exercise area? Are the runs big enough? Is there a space where the dog can get out of the sight of the other dogs? Is it heated and air conditioned? What is the daily cost? What do they require for vaccinations before boarding your dog? Is someone nearby during the night in case of any problems?

Hiring a pet sitter might be more expensive per day (sometimes not), but your animal will be in his own home and be more relaxed. Pet sitters should belong to an organization that insures and bonds them. Ask for references. Will they also bring in your mail and turn the lights on during one visit and off the next? Will they take Spike for a walk and spend some time with him? Have the pet sitter come to your house and see how well he/she gets along with Spike. How does Spike react to the sitter? Sometimes, you can get a friend or a friend's older child to watch Spike. A gift certificate to a good restaurant or business is a great way to say Thank You.

Make sure the pet sitter has the phone number of where you will be, that of someone close by to help in case of an emergency, and the vet's. You should also leave a list of any known allergies, the feeding schedule, and how and when to give any medications.

Call several veterinarian offices in the area and ask what boarding or pet sitting services they recommend. If you have four of the same referrals from vets within a twenty-mile radius, then that usually says something good about the referrals. Even if the sitter sounds good on the telephone, make an appointment to meet with him/her. In the case of a boarding kennel, go see the facility. Sometimes doing so without advanced warning may reveal their true colors. First thing in the morning, right before and after feeding times, and toward the end of the day, any boarding kennel will have its share of messes and smells not present during the rest of the day. If you visit during those times, take what you see with a grain of salt. In the case of a pet sitter, see if he/she will come to your house. That way there will be no surprises. The pet sitter can't say at the last minute, "I didn't think your house was so far from me," leaving you scrambling to have Spike taken care of. You can also see how well Spike relates to the sitter and vice versa.

Make sure the dog walker is insured and bonded so that he/she is responsible for any damage Spike might do while out on a walk. For a working person, a dog walker will ensure that a dog does not stay in a crate for too long a time. In fact, it is almost a necessity if you have a young dog and work full-time. Until Spike is old enough to trust alone in the house, you will need either to go home during your lunch break (to let him out to go to the bathroom and get some exercise) or to hire a dog walker. If you do not know of a dog walker in your area, call your veterinarian and see if he/she knows of one. If the vet does not, call the high school and see if a student who is used to dogs would like to earn some money. Get references from his/her teacher, neighbors, and friends so that you feel okay leaving Spike in his/her care.

Drop in unexpectedly at a day care facility, just as you would for a boarding kennel. How many dogs does one person watch out for and take care of? Are twenty to forty dogs allowed to run around together? Is there a separate playtime or area for young puppies and smaller dogs? Is there any naptime or downtime? How soon after meals do they allow the animals to interact again? Can you drop Spike off for a few hours, or do you need to bring him in for a day? If Spike is being trained, will the people help with his lessons? If so, what is the extra charge? Will they do the lessons the way you want them done or whatever way they want to? Will they try to make you believe that their way is best (maybe it is, maybe it isn't)? Does the place look and smell fairly clean? (There will always be some "doggy'" odor.)

There are pros and cons to any situation, including boarding Spike or taking him to day care. In a kennel, dogs usually are more stressed and do not eat as well. And there is the possibility of Spike coming home with fleas, ear mites, kennel cough, or other problems.

With day care, the caregivers may have too many animals to take care of or watch properly. Is Spike being picked on or picking on another dog and is not being helped or stopped in time? If too many dogs run together on a regular basis, a pack or two will be formed. One pack could challenge the other pack of dogs. Having too many dogs play together only invites accidents and problems. If dogs are allowed to play together all day, Spike will be a very tired dog when he gets home, but he will be learning to go all day during the daytime. That's not what you want when it is raining out and you have a day off. Nap times are necessary for all dogs, regardless of age. It also gives the caregivers a breather.

If they feed Spike and then almost immediately let him have playtime, the chances for an upset stomach or even a gastric torsion are greater. While generally the giant breeds are more prone to gastric torsions, small breeds have had them, even ten-pound terriers.

If Spike only goes to the day care facility once a week and most of the other dogs go more often, he may be picked on for being "the new kid on the block." To prevent that from happening, he should go to day care at least twice a week.

If you want Spike to have some training while he is at day care, be prepared to pay extra for it—after all Spike will be getting extra attention and time spent on him. Make sure they understand and will carry out the way you want Spike handled and trained.

No matter how many times a week Spike goes to a day care facility, he is almost guaranteed to come home tired. This may be good in cases where you have a busy family life or evening activities. But what if that is the time you usually spend bonding with Spike or training him? He will be too tired to pay attention to almost anything, even if you wave steak in front of his face. If you want the best of both worlds, take Spike to day care two to three times a week and train him the days he stays home.

If you cannot find a day care center, consider whether you live in an area that might support one and start your own business!

One final note of caution: If you are planning to be away in the near future, now is not the time to change Spike's diet. Between changing his diet and the stress of you being gone, he may end up with diarrhea.

Chapter 25

Traveling with Spike

If traveling for any distance in a car, do not give Spike food or water within three hours of departure. Once you have been driving for a few hours, take a break and give Spike a little water to drink. Take him for a walk and let him stretch his legs. Once you have stopped driving for the day, let Spike relax and adjust to his new surroundings before feeding him. Otherwise, you will increase the chances of him having an upset stomach.

Make sure Spike is safe and secure in your vehicle. This could mean that Spike rides in a crate, in a doggy seat belt, or behind a barrier. Bring along a favorite toy so that Spike will feel more at home. It will also help keep him occupied.

As stated in a previous chapter, letting a dog ride loose in the back of a pickup truck is like playing Russian roulette. Sooner or later, Spike will fall out of the back or over the side when you hit the brakes suddenly. Even if he does not get hit by a car, he could break a leg or worse from hitting the ground so sharply. Having a dog tied while in the back of a pickup truck is better than nothing, but if the line is too long, Spike may go over the side and strangle or be dragged. There is no shade in the back of an open pickup and, despite the breeze made by the moving vehicle, Spike can get heatstroke from the sun. He MUST have shade and water available, or he could dehydrate quite rapidly. In some states, it is illegal to have a dog in the back of a pickup unless there is a cap on the truck.

Dogs riding loose inside of cars can be bounced around if you put the brakes on suddenly. Small dogs may even become airborne and slam into the dashboard of the car, injuring themselves.

If your vehicle is large enough, put Spike in a crate in the car or in the back of the truck. If your car is not big enough for a crate, go to your local pet store or order a doggy seat belt. These seat belts come in a variety of sizes, so you will need to know how to measure Spike to get the right fit. People in the pet store or the catalog company can tell you what measurements you will need to be able to order the right size.

Car barriers are made to fit most cars, wagons, vans, and jeeps. They are made of metal pieces that make a partition, with Spike on one side and people on the other. Spike can get too hot behind a barrier that makes him stay in the back of the vehicle with the sun glaring down on him. Provide him with shade and good air circulation when using this type of barrier. Good air circulation does not mean riding with his head out the car window. It only takes a very small stone bounced up by a passing car to leave Spike blind in one eye. If you have ever ridden a bicycle down a hill at top speed and been hit in the face or eye by a bug, you know it hurts! Since it's difficult to put glasses or goggles on

Spike to protect his eyes when his head is out the window, keep his head in the car. Better safe then sorry.

Check ahead of time what motels along your route will accept dogs. Bringing a crate for him to be in while in the motel room will increase your chances of finding lodging.

Bring a large chew toy for Spike to have while in the motel room. If he is busy chewing on that, he will usually stay quiet while you go out for supper. If possible, bring the blanket, towel, or rug that Spike sleeps on at home. Being able to sleep on something that is familiar and smelling of home will help Spike relax faster in a new place.

Tranquilizers will keep Spike quiet for the ride, but they MUST be administered at least an hour before you put him in the car. If Spike senses something is happening and starts to get edgy a few hours before you take off, give him the tranquilizer. Otherwise once Spike gets stressed out, he will fight off the effects of the tranquilizer and be nervous the whole trip. Once he is settled for the rest of the day, he will "crash" and sleep for a long time.

If Spike is prone to carsickness, he can be taught to accept traveling in a vehicle and be less stressed. Again, don't feed Spike for at least three hours before you take him for a trip around the block. If he does not do well with that short a trip, make the next one even shorter. The more times he can go for a short ride and not get sick, the faster he will get over this problem. You can give him Dramamine about an hour before taking him on a longer trip. This medication may make him drowsy for several hours. Another human medication for the same problem is called Bonine. This medicine does not make humans or animals sleepy.

Flying Spike has some risk during certain times of the year. Most airlines will not accept Spike during days with temperatures of eight-five degrees or higher or temperatures of thirty-five degrees or less. Giving Spike a tranquilizer for flying may make matters worse. When Spike is tranquilized, he cannot regulate his body temperature as accurately. He will go into heatstroke faster in warmer temperatures or become too cold in colder climates. Just as panting in hot weather results in a little weight loss for Spike, so does shivering in cold weather. In extreme temperatures either way, dogs may go into shock.

When flying Spike, try to get as direct a route to the destination as possible. If there is a layover of over forty-five minutes and the weather is too hot or too cold at THAT airport, airlines do not have to allow Spike to continue on, even if YOU are on board. And remember that Spike will need to have a health certificate from his veterinarian within a week of his flying.

Whatever mode of transportation you take with Spike, you should have written instructions with you. These would include how you want him cared for if something should happen to you, who to contact to pick him up, who is to keep him, what he is being fed, the dates of his last vaccinations, who his regular veterinarian is, any allergies, and any medication Spike may be taking on a regular basis. Having a will that states what should be done with Spike on file with your attorney is great, but it does not help Spike if something should happen to you when you are away from home. Telling friends or family members will usually take care of Spike's immediate needs, but if there is any dissension within the family, you may want to leave a written statement with a friend.

Chapter 26

If You Can't Keep Spike

Sometimes, even if we don't want them to, our lives change. It could be a new job, a new baby, a move, or an injury. Sometimes Spike can to be relegated to the "back burner" and ignored for a while. But left to his own devices for too long, Spike will turn into a dog no one wants to have around.

Sometimes you get a puppy/dog for all of the right reasons, but the dog is not right for you. Watching Border collies work sheep is awe inspiring. But try to live with one. These dogs have been bred to work eight to twelve hours (at least) a day. They are not suited to being a couch potato and going for one run a day, no matter how long or far. Did you want a hunting dog who would be active in the field and flush as much game as possible or retrieve until you called it quits? How long is hunting season versus the time the dog spends at home waiting for the next season to start? The dog on *Frasier* is cute; but Jack Russell terriers are called "perpetual motion" for a reason. Some mixed breeds are not fun either. Take a Labrador retriever crossed with a Siberian husky. One side of the dog wants to be with his owners; the other half wants to go out and run as far and as fast as he can. Unless you are a really active person, this mixed breed is not suitable for most people.

Tying Spike outside (weather permitting) is not the way to deal with the issue. Keeping him crated in the house with just time to go outside and play is not the way to handle it either. Both solutions will usually create more problems than they solve.

Whether you are by yourself or have a family, a decision has to be made as to what is best for Spike. Is this just a temporary problem? Will you be able to spend more time with Spike in the near future? Can a relative take him for a few weeks or a month?

All too often, children or grandchildren decide that their parents or grandparents need a dog, and they get them a puppy. But some older people would do much better with a middle-aged dog.

Sometimes it is better for all concerned to realize that a particular dog is not right for you. Where does Spike go if you have made the decision that it is best for him to leave you?

Trying to Place Spike Yourself

The first choice is to call the person you got him from, no matter how long ago that was. While they are in the minority right now, some breeders will always take back their offspring, regardless of how old or in what condition. They want to know and account for all the puppies their dogs had.

If the person who had the litter will not take the dog back, do you have a friend interested in taking Spike? Tack up an ad with a picture at the local animal hospitals. Go in and talk to the receptionists at these places. Sometimes they know of someone who lost a dog recently and is looking for another. Be honest about Spike, both his good points and his bad habits. Otherwise, you will be receiving a phone call within a few weeks asking if you will take him back.

If you are going to try and place Spike in a new home yourself, be picky. Ask for references. If they had animals in the past, ask what animal hospital they took them to. Call and ask if these people took good care of their animals. You don't have to know the whole history, but did they get the vaccinations done on time? Was the animal ever denied any procedure? Make sure it is a good home. Otherwise Spike will be passed on to someone else in a few short months.

How and where will they be exercising Spike? Do they have a fenced-in yard, or do they live on a very busy street? Would they take the dog for walks every day, even sometimes two to three times a day? Are there any children? If Spike does not get along with children, he should not go to a new family with children in hopes that in his new home he will learn to get along with them. Usually the opposite is true; if he is upset and confused by his new surroundings, he may lash out even faster at a child.

Do they have any other animals? How is Spike with other animals? If he has never met a cat, let the potential new owners know so that they can prepare for dealing with the issue.

Also, don't be afraid to ask for some money. After all, if Spike has been house-trained, vaccinated, neutered, and trained, he should not go for free. Who really appreciates or takes care of anything they got for free? That does not mean you should charge hundreds of dollars for Spike. Charge just enough to show the new family that Spike means something to you and to ensure that Spike will mean something to them.

Even though it will be hard, especially if you have children, do not go and visit Spike in his new home more than once. To do it more would only upset Spike and your children. He needs to learn to settle in with his new owners. Your children need to learn that Spike is in his new home and that they are not a part of his life anymore.

Be honest with your children! Even though they will be hurt in the beginning, they will remember that you were honest with them. To lie to them about what happened to Spike will only cause problems as they grow up and begin to understand about life and choices.

Living near the beach, we have a number of kittens and puppies left after every summer. People get the animals for their children while they are here on vacation and then realize that they have no room for them back in the city. Sometimes these young animals find new homes; other times they make up feral packs and run wild, waiting for handouts from humans.

Breed Rescue Organizations

There are breed rescue organizations for almost every breed of dog in the United States and Canada. Almost every humane shelter will be able to find the contact person or telephone number for your particular breed of dog. Some animal hospitals may have the information also.

These people are committed to trying to find each dog the right home, not just the first family available at the time. They do home studies on the potential new family or person. They find out how active that person or family is, how much time they can give to the animal, whether they can afford the animal's upkeep, and so on. Then they as closely as possible match up a dog for them. Maybe it is your dog, maybe it is one who has been waiting months for a home.

Once the dog has been turned over to the breed rescue person, it is usually put in either a foster home or a boarding kennel, usually one that belongs to a person who raises that particular breed—so he/she knows the temperament, quirks, and so on, of that breed. These people do home studies, transport dogs, foster them, board them, train them, get them veterinary care, and get very little, if any, money for doing so. They do it because they want to help that breed.

These organizations keep afloat through donations. They may ask you for a donation when you give up Spike to them. It is one way to cover part of his upkeep until they find him a new home or to pay for the upkeep of an animal who needs more veterinary care.

Humane Shelters

For a long time, shelters have been a place to drop off all kinds of animals that no one wants anymore. Some have been abused or ill and, through these shelters, have received care and found loving homes.

However, most shelters have become overcrowded, perhaps because of the population growth of the animals and humans. They try to do what is right for the animals as much as they can.

Some shelters have a "no kill" policy, which at first sounds great. No animal is put to sleep; they try to find all animals a home no matter how long it takes. But what if Spike is not social with other dogs? He'll have them on both sides of him, in a run, all day long, running and snarling at each other, day after day. This is not going to turn him into a dog lover. Or what if Spike is high strung or stresses easily? Eventually he will settle into the routine of the place, but each time a new dog shows up on one side of him or the other, throughout his stay there, he will probably stress out. This is certainly not a great life for Spike.

On the other hand, some shelters are so busy that they can only keep animals for two to three weeks before having them put to sleep. What is best for your Spike?

Shelters, like breed rescue organizations, are run mostly by volunteers. Do not be surprised if you are asked for a donation when you drop Spike off. Also, be honest with his good and bad habits. This way they can do a better job at matching him up with a potential new home. Better that he wait a few weeks for the right home than to be in a new home every four months because no one wants to deal with his annoying or bad habits.

Both breed rescue organizations and humane shelters do the best that they can. They both exist solely from donations, yet they do so much good work. If you can't give a donation, try to volunteer. They can use all the help they can get.

Euthanasia

This subject is included as a way to resolve the issue of where does Spike go from here? While it is never a first choice, for a dog with a lot of medical or behavioral problems, it may be the wisest choice in the long run. If you, the one who raised Spike, don't want to deal with his medical bills or his behavioral problems, what makes you think someone else will? Maybe Spike needs monthly blood work or expensive surgery. Most people don't want to start off with a dog who has higher monthly medical expenses than they do.

What if Spike has some aggression problems? Or what if you didn't take the time to teach him what was appropriate and what was not? Again, few people want to start off with such a dog.

If you have a dog who has bitten anyone, think real hard about whether to place that dog or have him put to sleep. In some states, it is illegal for shelters, rescue organizations, or private citizens to adopt or be given a dog who has bitten, regardless of the reason why he bit. If such a dog bites someone again, the person who is bitten can sue the original owner.

A dog who has bitten more than twice is usually confirmed as a biter. He is like a loaded pistol just waiting to go off. You don't know when, who, or why; you just know that he will bite someone again.

There are exceptions, and you would need the help of a VERY experienced behaviorist to turn this type of dog around. Plus you would have to be committed, above all else, to spending the time and energy and patience needed to do the retraining.

Chapter 27

Conclusion

Raising a puppy is a lot like raising a child. You invest a lot of time, love, energy, and patience, patience, patience. The more you invest in the beginning, the more you get back as the dog grows and matures into the kind of dog you can take places and have people admire.

You need a sense of humor also; sometimes it's better to laugh than to get so upset that you ruin your relationship with Spike. Once a dog has gotten you to laugh at him, he will find ways to have you repeat this as often as possible. Laughter is supposed to be the best medicine. So enjoy your dog as much as possible.

There are many different ways to raise a dog. If you go to the bookstore and check out the animal section, you will find a book on every method out there. Just for curiosity sake, check out the section on raising children. Twenty years ago, there would have been more books on how to raise a puppy than on how to raise a child.

You need to raise Spike in a manner that is right for you and your family. Maybe there are a few parts in this book that you don't agree with. That's okay; you don't have to agree 100 percent. I just want you to be able to make choices and know what is out there for choices.

If you keep an open mind, your dog will tell you what methods work best with him. When I first started to raise puppies from those super well-trained obedience-titled dogs, I could not understand why the puppies I kept from the litters were so stupid—they would get into the trash bin, chew on something inappropriate, run around the house knocking over people and furniture. Then I took a step back and realized that *I* was the problem! Any time an older dog did any of those things, I had gone ballistic, and the puppies had gotten a very clear picture of what set me off. Whenever they were bored, they would try one of these "tricks" to see if I would react in my old manner. Once I realized that I was at the root of the problem, I started to really praise the older dogs lavishly whenever they did anything I liked and tried to ignore as much as possible anything I did not like. When I did feel the need to correct, I did so with a quiet but firm tone of voice, with the silent treatment, or with a time-out. Both the older dogs and the puppies responded like sponges, soaking it all in, and within months, I had much better responding dogs and MUCH better behaved puppies.

The moral of this story is simple: We usually cause the very problems we are trying to avoid—by using poor judgment and poor correction techniques.

Dogs have been known to save their owners' lives. This is not uncommon. Any dog that has a good relationship with his owner would do this if and when the need arose. There are many books on the subject. Just watch Spike when you bring a new-born baby into the house. Most dogs will lie underneath the bassinet or crib just to make sure no one gets too close to the baby without Mom's or Dad's permission.

We had a super little thirty-pound mutt who would vacate the area when company arrived, until we had a newborn. Then she was always near the baby, ready to protect him. I could leave the baby in the car seat and go into a store for a few minutes, knowing that Seymour would give up her life before she would let any harm come to Adam. This dog was six years old when I married my husband, and we did not always have the best of rela-tionships. But when I came home from the hospital five years later with a baby, she became "The Guardian." She looked out for Adam and me. I miss her still. Stormy taught Adam how to walk—he held onto her back and she would get up and slowly walk in a straight line until he had had enough.

Dogs are ever ready to do our bidding. They are ever ready to listen to us and hear our fears, our complaints. They do not judge; they just are. They can enrich our lives tremendously if we let them.

Any of you who watch the annual Westminster Dog Show at Madison Square Garden in New York City in February know the voice of Roger Caras. He announces each breed and tells a little about it. He sits on the board of quite a few humane shelters and also has written a few books about dogs. This passage is taken from *A Celebration of Dogs:*

> Dogs have always subsisted on handouts. We give them
> the love we can spare, the time we can spare, the room
> we can spare. Even the best of the balanced dog foods,

although meticulously compounded, consist of what we can spare from the slaughterhouse and what we can grow on the land we can spare. In return, dogs have given us their absolute all. We are the center of their universe, we are the focus of their love and faith and trust. They serve us in return for scraps. It is without doubt the best deal man has ever made.

Tribute to a Dog

The one absolutely unselfish friend that man can have in this selfish world, the one that never deserts him, the one that never proves ungrateful or treacherous, is his dog. A man's dog stands by him in prosperity and in poverty, in health and in sickness. He will sleep on the cold ground, where the wintry winds blow and the snow drives fiercely, if only he may be near his master's side. He will kiss the hand that has no food to offer; he will lick the wounds and sores that come in encounter with the roughness of the world. He guards the sleep of his pauper master as if he were a prince. When all other friends desert, he remains. When riches take wings and reputation falls to pieces, he is as constant in his love as the sun in its journey through the heavens.

By Senator George Vest, 1870

Where to Find Supplies and Information

The following pet supply catalogs offer good quality items at discount prices:

R. C. Steele, 1-800-872-3773, $50 minimum order
J-B Wholesale, 1-800-526-0388, $25 minimum order
New England Serum Co., 1-800-637-3786
Drs. Foster & Smith, 1-800-826-7206
The Dog's Outfitter, 1-800-367-3647
Pets USA, 1-800-473-8872

Direct Book Service has a great catalog of dog and cat titles. They range from specific breeds, to health, holistic care, feeding, training, behavior, and just stories. The number is 800-776-2665.

4-M Enterprises also carries a full line of books, plus quite a few that are out of print. The number is 800-487-9867.

To inquire about obedience and/or breed clubs in your area, contact your veterinarian. Also check the local papers and TV to find out the dates of any local dog shows. Or write to the AKC:

The American Kennel Club
5580 Centerview Drive
Raleigh, NC 27690-0643
Web site http://www.akc.org

The AKC can also give you copies of their rules and regulations for showing a dog to obtaining titles in breed confirmation, obedience, tracking, agility, herding, and hunting.

AMBOR is an organization that registers mixed breeds. They also award titles for the same competitions as the AKC.

AMBOR
P.O. Box 7841
Rockford, IL 61126-7841
815-874-2909

The United Kennel Club recognizes some breeds that the AKC does not. They also offer titles, but they have different requirements.

United Kennel Club
100 East Kilgore Road
Kalamazoo, MI 49001-5587
616-343-9020

There are magazines devoted to a single breed or to several breeds with common interests such as herding, hunting, or terrier work. Check with your local bookstore and pick up a copy of *Dog World* or *Dog Fancy*. These publications provide lots of information and, in some cases, advertise individual breed magazines.

The AKC also publishes a monthly magazine, called the *AKC Gazette,* with articles on obedience, breeding, behavior, showing, field work, and so on, along with monthly columns on individual breeds.

The Canadian Kennel Club has a monthly magazine called *Dogs in Canada.* Contact them for a subscription:
Canadian Kennel Club
100-89 Skyway Avenue
Etobicoke, Ontario M9W 6R4
416-675-3944

The National Dog Registry, among others, will register tattooed dogs:
National Dog Registry
P.O. Box 116
Woodstock, NY 12498-0116
They can also give you a list of people in your area who do tattooing for them.

Here are two organizations that register therapy dogs:

Therapy Dogs Inc.
P.O. Box 5868
Cheyenne, WY 82003
877-843-7364

Therapy Dogs International
6 Hilltop Road
Mendham, NJ 07945
201-543-0888

To find holistic veterinarians contact these organizations:

American Holistic Veterinary Medical Association
2214 Old Emmorton Road
Bel Air, MD 21015
410-569-0795

American Veterinary Chiropractic Association
623 Main
Hillsdale, IL 61257
309-658-2920

Center for Veterinary Acupuncture
Maria Glinski, DVM
1405 W. Silver Spring Drive
Glendale, WI 53209
800-680-2282

International Veterinary Acupuncture Society
P.O. Box 2074
Nederland, CO 80466-2074
303-658-2920

The specialty foods mentioned in the book can be found through advertisements in either *Dog World* and/or *Dog Fancy*. Both are sold at most book and magazine stores.
There are many good books on the market covering training, behavior, health, nutrition, working, fun, and so on. Some of the better books may not be on the bookstore shelves, but they can be ordered through Direct Book Service or 4-M Enterprises (see "Where to Find Supplies and Information" section).

Book List

The following is only a partial list. You may have to read a few to find one that suits the way you want to train your dog. (They all have good information.)

Making Friends by Linda Colflesh
Dog Training for Kids by Carol Lea Benjamin
Family Dog by Richard Wolters
The Dog's Mind by Dr. Bruce Fogle
Pooches & Small Fry (Parenting skills for dogs and kids!) by Jack and Colleen McDaniel
Just Say "Good Dog" by Linda Goodman
Playtraining Your Dog by Patricia Gail Burnham
What All Good Dogs Should Know by Jack Volhard and Melissa Bartlett
Training Your Dog by John Rogerson
Why Does My Dog ...? By John Fisher

Good Owners Great Dogs by Brian Kilcommons

Surviving Your Dog's Adolescence by Carol Lea Benjamin

Natural Health for Dogs & Cats by Dr. Richard Pitcairn

Tellington Touch by Linda Tellington-Jones and Taylor

Enjoying Dog Agility by Julie Daniels

Fun Nosework for Dogs by Roy Hunter

Practical Scent Dog Training by Lou Button

Dog Tricks by Capt. Arthur Haggerty and Carol Lea Benjamin

Child Proofing Your Dog by Brian Kilcommons and Sarah
   Wilson

Mother Knows Best, The Natural Way to Train Your Dog by
   Carol Lea Benjamin

Lads Before the Wind by Karen Pryor

Behavior Problems in Dogs by William Campbell

Owner's Guide to Dog Health by Lowell Ackerman, DVM

Dogs: Homeopathic Remedies by George Macleod, MRCVS,
   DVSM

The Homeopathic Treatment of Small Animals by Christopher
   Day

Love, Miracles, and Animal Healing by Allen M. Schoen,
   DVM, and Pan Proctor

The Holistic Guide for a Healthy Dog by Wendy Volhard and
   Kerry Brown, DVM

The following books are helpful if you want to make your own
dog food. You can find them at your bookstore:

It's for the Animals Cook Book and Resource Directory by
   Helen McKinnon

Food Pets Die For by Anne Martin.

Give Your Dog a Bone by Ian Billinghurst, BVSc(Hons),
   BScAgr, DipEd

Grow Your Pups with Bones by Ian Billinghurst, BVSc(Hons), BScAgr, DipEd
Foods That Heal by Dr. Bernard Jensen
Prescription for Nutritional Healing by James F. Balch, M.D., and Phyllis A. Balch, C.N.C

Here are two new additions to the book list. (These are excellent books but you may only find them at Howln Moon Press, 203 State Road, Eliot, ME 03909, 207-439-3508.)

Your Dog and Your Baby by Silvia Hartmann-Kent
Training Your Dog with Love by Silvia Hartmann-Kent

Index

About the Author

MARY THOMPSON lives in York, Maine, with her veterinarian husband, Ross and son Adam. (Andrew is old enough to have left the nest.) Mary started training dogs when she was fourteen. She took her love of animals and made a career out of it by going to the second largest animal hospital in the world, Angell Memorial Animal Hospital in Boston, MA, to be trained as a veterinary technician. She has been a practicing veterinary technician since 1970 and licensed in the state of Maine since 1978.

In 1977 Mary and Ross opened a small animal hospital. They also started a new business called Fresh Start in 1992. They offer public obedience classes, private lessons, behavior consultation, and boarding and training.

Mary has been involved in LRR, Inc. (Labrador Retriever Rescue, Inc.) for many years. She has owned, raised, bred, and shown Labrador retrievers for over twenty years. Her dogs have won championships and obedience titles in both the United States and Canada. Each of the dogs who competed for obedience titles has earned Highest Scoring Labrador retriever and, sometimes, Highest Scoring Sporting Dog. They have also earned tracking titles in the United States. One of her Labs, Storm, was the town's first police tracking dog. Storm found or assisted in the finding of three lost children and eight wanted people.

She now raises Irish water spaniels and has a whippet. Son Adam raised and trained his Norwich terrier from the time he was ten. All her dogs are registered Therapy Dogs and visit nursing homes, hospitals, and schools. Mary has started a children's school program in her town and the surrounding towns with her dogs and human friends.

Mary has been an obedience instructor since 1981 and has attended many seminars on obedience training, behavior consulting, health, nutrition, and orthopedic problems. She has been judging match shows in both breed and obedience since 1983. Mary is an AKC and TDX licensed tracking judge and a provisional tracking judge for VST.

Fun activities with her dogs include field training, tracking, walking with friends and their dogs, agility, flyball, and getting together in front of the fireplace with the family on a cold winter night with a bowl of popcorn.

"My dogs are my friends—first, last, and always," she says. "What titles we have won have been achieved through work, patience, time, and fun. If you don't make training fun for your dog, the dog will work anyway. But what enjoyment will you get out of it if his tail isn't wagging?"

273

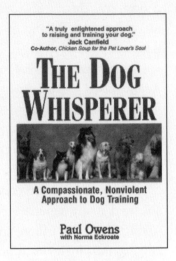